CHIME IN
Teacher Resource Guide

CHIME IN
Teacher Resource Guide

Jean Malloch

MAXWELL MACMILLAN CANADA

Edited by Marion E. Raycheba
Designed by John Zehethofer
Line Illustrations by Robert Brown and Associates
Music Illustrations by Musictype Limited

Published by
Maxwell Macmillan Canada
1200 Eglinton Ave., East
Don Mills, Ontario
M3C 3N1

7 8 9 95 94 93

ISBN 02.953785.1

Written, Printed and Bound in Canada

Contents

Foreword

Chime In has been written to satisfy the needs of teachers who are interested in providing a non-prescriptive, integrated program and in putting into practice the psycholinguistic theory of reading. It was developed over a period of ten years and piloted in ten schools with the co-operation of teachers whose teaching experience at the primary level varied considerably.

Children have many skills which they use in making sense of their world. *Chime In* capitalizes on these skills by suggesting open-ended activities which will awaken a child's curiosity and stimulate the search for answers.

Rather than presenting reading as a segmented and analytical skill, *Chime In* presents reading as a meaningful language process through literature and song. The child is free to develop competence and understanding at his or her own pace and in a way suited to his or her individual needs.

It is hoped that the program will be helpful to teachers and will bring joy and satisfaction to young learners.

Acknowledgements

It is with gratitude that I acknowledge Cindy Willcocks' illustrations of the mterials which were used in the pilot study, Bob Barton's suggestions of children's literature and the title for this series and Kitty Henderson's typing of the original drafts of the Teacher Resource Guide.

Many Program Leaders including Beth MacRae (Music), Dianne Domelle (Physical Education), Marilyn Hardie (Music) and Martha Serson (Art) were involved in presenting the program to teachers.

My friend, the late Lois Swain, will be remembered for her encouragement and for her professional advice.

Special thanks are due to my husband, Ian, for his understanding and support.

Many traditional songs and poems were used along with the following for which permission was kindly granted.
"Walk to School" by Mary Jaye.
"Stop! Look! Listen!" by John S. Murray.
"The End" by A.A. Milne.
"Happy Birthday" by Patty Smith
"Witch, Witch" by Rose Fyleman.
"Hannukah Lights" from *Rhymes for Fingers and Flannelboards*.

"One Red Spot" by Sheila Malloch.
"Five Kites" by Lucille Wood.
"Fire! Fire!" from *This is Music*.
"The Wind Blow East" from *Our Singing Country*.
"Going On a Picnic" by Garlid and Olson.
"Johnny Get Your Hair Cut" from *Hill Country Tunes* by S.P. Bayard.

Jean Malloch

Introduction

What Is Chime In?

Chime In is a collection of poems and songs to be used as the basis for a non-prescriptive, integrated program. Each theme is introduced by a poem or song, then expanded through activities related to language, mathematics, art, drama, environmental studies, music, and physical education.

Integration is more than tying subjects together with a theme. The teacher must provide experiences that will allow children not only to integrate subject matter but also, and more importantly, to integrate their perceptions. To accomplish this, the total organism must be involved — eyes, ears, voice, body movement, and emotions. The activities suggested in *Chime In*, therefore, incorporate a variety of media and encourage children to observe, organize, hypothesize, solve problems, create, and evaluate. Most activities are open-ended so that children are free to use their developing skills and to try out new ideas.

What Does Chime In Offer?

Chime In provides a beginning reading program for use in place of the traditional pre-primer and primer approach. The development of reading competence is best achieved when the learner's focus is on the message rather than on the decoding process. Dr. Yetta Goodman[1] has shown that children who are reading fully formed language will draw on syntactic and semantic information at very early stages in reading. In *Chime In*, every poem or song will be experienced in many ways so that the children will learn it well

[1] As reported by Kenneth Goodman in "Reading: a Psycholinguistic Guessing Game", *Theoretical Models and Processes of Reading*, edited by H. Singer and R. Riddell and published by the International Reading Association, 1976.

before the printed material is introduced. Comprehension no longer poses a problem, and children are free to focus on learning "how to read". Since the rhythm of word patterns and simple melodies makes repetition enjoyable, the children will have many opportunities to develop and practise their own ways of internalizing sentence patterns, words, and letters.

Chime In invites the child to read. As the teacher or parent chants and sings with the children, language comes alive. Suddenly, the marks on the page become meaningful because the message has become part of their experience. They have been reached emotionally and intellectually. Since real learning involves both of these faculties — the emotion and the intellect — the classroom becomes a place where children may "live" the poems, songs, and stories.

Chime In builds children's language resources. Favourite stories can be read over and over again until the children feel the emotions expressed and until the beauty of the language becomes their language, too. It has been said that the ability to read today depends on what we have heard and experienced in all our yesterdays. This may also be said of children's ability to write creatively and expressively. What has been heard and experienced enriches their vocabulary and guides their use of punctuation. The rhythm of poetry and song helps children to develop their awareness of sentence and phrase and also provides a pattern for their own attempts at writing.

Chime In creates a happy classroom environment and ensures that every child will experience a feeling of success. When chanting or singing, the children have many opportunities to practise reading in an atmosphere where there is no price tag of right or wrong. Any anxiety that may hinder learning is avoided.

Most reading programs require children to

learn a certain number of words *before* they are able or allowed to proceed to the next story. In the *Chime In* program, every child moves on to the next poem regardless of the number of words he or she is able to recognize. For example, one child may be able to read all the words, another may recognize five, another two, and another none at all. The child who is not able to recognize isolated words will still be developing *other* reading skills, such as acquiring a feeling for sentences and phrases and learning to make hypotheses, to predict, and to listen. It is important to foster the development of these skills by introducing new materials and activities rather than by drilling the same material over and over again.

Chime In provides a plethora of poems, songs, and story suggestions to stimulate the attention and interest of the children so that each child will learn what he or she is ready to learn. Individual differences in skill and development are accommodated in the follow-up activities.

Chime In Is Flexible

Chime In is a program which teachers may extend or adapt in their own way. It is not necessary to use every poem or song, nor is it necessary to use them in the order given. Teachers should, however, follow the method in the sequence given. For example, if a non-reader enters the class in January, he or she should be taught the Winter poems along with the other children. But the non-reader should also be encouraged to engage in activities appropriate for beginning readers in order to build self-confidence. Other children may be more able readers. In these cases, the teacher should choose a book or story related to the theme as their reading material. Suggestions are given on p. 8 for introducing children to books. As a general rule, it is more important to choose a book related to the theme than to follow a sequence of readers with controlled vocabulary.

Chime In is ideal for introducing reading to students learning English as a second language. It is important for these children to respond to the rhythm and intonation of the language through movement before focusing on the meaning of individual words. Their parents should continue to read to them and converse with them in their mother tongue.

Parents could also be encouraged to print and/or tape (in the mother tongue) poems and songs that are familiar to their children. These indigenous resources can be used as the children's reading programs until the concept of reading is established and the students have become more competent and fluent in English. The *Chime In* poems and songs may then be introduced. As they become familiar and welcome friends, they too may be introduced to the students in printed form.

Chime In is ideal for Special Education programs. For children who need longer to grasp the concept of reading, the poems or songs add variety and interest. The selections in *Chime In* may be varied or supplemented with others of the teacher's own choosing. For children with learning disabilities, *Chime In* allows scope to develop individual strategies for learning. In most cases, the primary child with special needs can be accommodated in a regular class if this or a similar program is used.

Blissymbols with Chime In

For a complete description of the use of Blissymbols with *Chime In*, see page 19.

Chime In in French

Chime In is also available in the French language. For *Tous ensemble*, the French-language program, the choice of poems and songs has been carefully considered. Most of these are traditional French *comptines*.

In addition to a teacher's guide, blackline masters, posters, and pupils' books, *Tous ensemble* includes an audio-cassette component. Each of the four cassettes is geared to two of the pupils' books.

Special Notes

Musical Accompaniment

Chime In does *not* require special musical ability or musical training on the part of the teacher. Melodies are given for the *Chime In* songs, but the songs may be treated as rhythmic poems.

Teachers who cannot read music but still wish to use a musical approach can accompany the songs on the autoharp. Anyone can use the autoharp with only a few minutes of self-instruction and practice. Try it for yourself with this simple song (sung to the tune of *London Bridge*). The song appears in this *Guide* with these autoharp key notations:

F
We are going to the zoo
C^7 F
To the zoo, to the zoo
We are going to the zoo
C^7 F
Won't you come along?

How to Play the Autoharp

1. Place the fingers of your left hand over the keys that you will need *before* beginning the song. (In this example, you will need keys F and C^7.) You will find that you do not need to watch your hands while playing.
2. Start playing by pressing the key marked F with the left hand. Sing the words while strumming the strings *from* lowest *to* highest with the right hand.
3. At the beginning of the second line, press the key marked C^7 and strum until F is shown.
4. At this point, press the F key while continuing to strum with the right hand.
5. Continue as marked.

Note: You will find that the keys needed for autoharp accompaniment are usually placed side by side. There will be no awkward stretches or difficult manoeuvres.

Selecting Poems and Songs

As you will see, this Guide includes 53 poems and songs divided into 13 theme units. Remember that the *Chime In* material is not to be regarded as prescriptive. Select for use only those poems and songs that you feel are best suited for your class. Add any others that you feel will interest the children and will complement your program. Easy books could also introduce a theme. These should be read several times to the children so that they will be able to read them as easily as they read the songs and poems.

Chime In Books

It is important — and will be a source of pride — for students to have, in their own hands, books that they can "read". Most children are excited by the concept of owning a book, whether or not they are able to read in the traditional sense of the word. Their pride in ownership will help stimulate their desire to read.

There are eight *Chime In* books. This *Guide* lists, on the title page of each theme, the book or books to be introduced.

As the children become familiar with the books, they should be displayed, along with other easy books, in the reading centre so that individual reading will be encouraged. Children love to read their favourites over and over again.

The children will enjoy reading their *Chime In* books to friends, visitors, or younger children. Experiencing this success will encourage them to enjoy books and also help develop self-confidence in reading.

Just as the teacher brings a small group together to read a novel, he or she should bring a group together to read their *Chime In* books. Beginning readers will then feel that they are participating successfully in the same type of activity as other children in their class.

Individualized Chime In Theme Books

You may also choose to make use of the Duplicating Masters which accompany *Chime In* to help create individualized *Chime In* theme books with your students. These will be useful for writing activities and will allow for more flexibility in programming.

1. Using the black line Duplicating Masters, duplicate each poem on paper punched for a 3-ringed binder. If possible, use a different colour of paper for each theme.
2. Give each child a loose-leaf, three-ringed binder in which to store the sheets as they are distributed.
3. Distribute individual copies *after* the song or poem has been taught. These could be illustrated by the children.
4. The children may add pages for additional verses which could be completed during writing activities.
5. Other work relating to the theme could be added — a story which the child has written, illustrations of stories which the teacher has read, pictures from newspapers or magazines, recordings of mathematical discoveries or illustrations of Social Studies or Science activities.

Children should be encouraged to take their *Chime In* booklets home as often as they wish to read to their parents. Teachers find that there is such a pride of ownership that very few of these booklets are lost. At the end of the unit or at the end of the year, the books may be kept by the students. These personalized "books" will be treasured by both the children and their parents.

Wall Charts and Posters

It is recommended that teachers purchase the 13 *Chime In* Posters, covering 16 poems and songs, or make their own wall charts by copying each poem or song on chart paper. These could be illustrated by the children and then laminated. Display the posters or wall charts of the songs or poems which have been taught. It is important to leave these on display even after moving on to a new theme. Teachers have found that children will use them as a resource for their writing activities. Posters and wall charts may also be used for shared reading or frequent reviews with either a small group or the entire class.

Activity Centres

There are many activities possible for each theme. In addition to those suggested in the *Guide*, consider alternatives from themes covered previously or develop additional activities.

Once an activity has been introduced and the children have learned the required routines, continue the activity as long as the children's interest lasts. Often, putting away an activity and then bringing it out again a few weeks later sparks renewed interest.

Set up various activity centres for language, writing, painting, blockbuilding, sand play, listening, drama, and so on. Place appropriate resource materials at each centre. For example, the language centre could have story books with records for listening, large picture books, alphabet puzzles, picture sets to arrange in sequence, a flannel board with stick-on figures, etc. The mathematics centre should contain games involving counting and adding, pegboards and blocks, number and shape puzzles, a flannel board with stick-on shapes and numbers, a magnetic board, balances, scales, and graph paper.

The illustration on page 6 shows how you might arrange activity centres within the typical classroom.

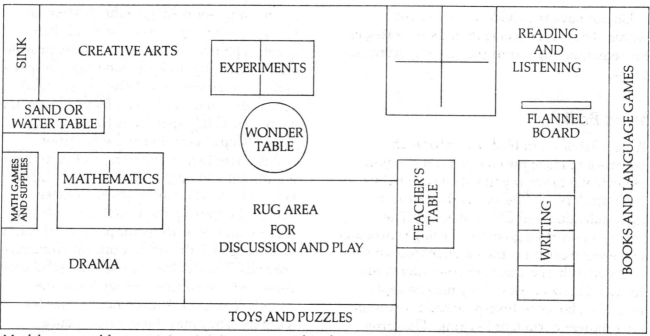

Model suggested for arranging activity centres within the typical classroom.

Making Sense of Print

Observing the Children

Take the time for careful observation while the children are involved in their activities, especially play and choice activities. Your observations will tell you what strategies they are using to make sense of print. For example, you may hear a child say, "This is a long word," or "This word looks the same as ____ ". Some children may begin copying words and asking what they mean, while others may be colouring all the similar words in their individualized *Chime In* books. Children who are showing such interest are ready to begin building word banks.

Children who are having difficulty in recognizing words in isolation should not be involved in word bank activities. They may be younger than their classmates or developing more slowly. There may be social or emotional problems which need attention. If they are enjoying "reading" the poems and are learning that print is meaningful, do not require more of them until they signal that they are ready.

Word Cards

For each song, the teacher could make sentence and phrase cards, punch them, and hook them with shower-curtain rings in the language arts centre. Children who are not ready to deal with individual word cards may arrange these phrase cards to match the wall chart. Teachers should also make individual word cards for each song or poem and store them in pockets underneath the wall charts or in a file or envelope on which a copy of the complete song or poem is mounted. Children may take these word cards and lay them on the phrase cards until they are ready to use them alone. When the children complete the song or poem, they should be encouraged to read or sing it with the teacher or a friend.

It is important to remember that we are encouraging children to start from a meaningful whole, to deal with parts, and finally to create the whole again.

Encourage those children who are ready to pick out specific words from the word-card stack. If the children cannot recognize the word in isolation, have them find it in the poem or song first and then select the word card.

Do not have the children "sound out" words. They will develop their own strategies for remembering words that are important to them.

Word Banks

Keep a list of scrambled words for each poem/song. Have the children come to you individually to show you which words they *know*. Underscore the words they *know* in their individualized *Chime In* books. The children may then go to the writing centre and make word cards for the underscored words.

Provide library, index, or computer cards for word bank entries. They may be kept in individual boxes or hole-punched for storage on a shower curtain or key ring. The cards should be stored in alphabetical order.

Review the word bank entries as often as possible with each child (preferably daily). Older students and parent volunteers may be of great help with this. Since only the words they *know* are on the cards, the children will develop confidence and will soon be ready to add families of words to the cards (for example, *day, say,* and *play* to the *may* word card).

Not every child in the class will be making word cards at the same time. Some may not be ready and those who are reading fluently will no longer need them. Word cards should only be used to support the child who is showing an interest in identifying words and becoming adept at finding words that rhyme.

Sound/Symbol Relationships

It has been said that children learn phonics through reading rather than reading through phonics (Dr. Frank Smith, Reading '72, York University).

When children have acquired some skill in phonics, they will begin making nonsense rhymes or noting similarities in sounds of words. Listen for these signals in their casual conversations.

The *Lappy Lappy* song (see p.60) and the *Ay Ay* song (see p.92) give the children an enjoyable way of practising some of their acquired phonic skills. The songs also provide for self-listening. Keep in mind that there is a neurological connection between the vocal apparatus and the inner ear. By producing the sound, the child experiences the reciprocal relationship of listening and articulation.

It is better to give children practice in their phonic skills by singing such songs as *Lappy Lappy* and *Ay Ay* than by giving written exercises requiring them to find words with specific sounds or to colour pictures of objects beginning with the same sound. Such exercises are tests. The children can be successful with these tests *only* if they already know the sounds. Thus, the tests do not provide for learning. They may, however, produce frustration in the children who are unable to complete them successfully.

In contrast, using songs provides auditory, visual, and vocal stimulation as well as enjoyment in repetition. Thus, a learning environment is established.

Beginning Writing

It is important that children feel that they can express themselves in writing. They should be involved in many kinds of writing and encouraged to use many strategies such as copying words from the songs and poems, guessing at spelling, or using their word banks.

It is common for children at the beginning of grade one to have a few words which they know how to write and also to have an awareness of initial consonants. At this stage they should be encouraged to print the initial consonant and then draw a line for the remainder of the word. Later, in conference with the teacher, they can fill the spaces in. One or two words which the child will likely be using often should be selected for discussion and then printed by the child in his or her dictionary.

The teacher may also find little stories useful in helping children to remember irregular spellings. For example, the silent *K* in the word *know* (*I Know a Little Pussy*, p.144) could be introduced as follows:

K was the laziest fellow. One day, he had to help say the word *keep*. He went to his friend, E, and said, "I'm too tired. Won't you talk for me?"

"No, sir!" said E. "You have to do your own work around here!"

The next day, K had to help with the word *know*. But he still felt tired, and so he went to his friend, N, and said, "Please talk for me."

"Well," said N, "You're a good friend. I'll talk for you."

So now, every time that K stands next to N, K doesn't have any work to do. N does it all.

Reading to Children

Since stories provide enrichment in vocabulary and expression, reading to the class is the best way to prepare children for reading on their own.

Suggestions for supplementary reading are listed throughout this *Guide*. Use your discretion. Read a variety of stories and poems, and be sure that some are selections that the children will be able to "read" as soon as they know the stories well. Cumulative stories or stories with a repeated chorus are particularly welcome because the children can join in, even during the first reading, as soon as they have discovered the pattern.

As you read, ask such questions as: What do you think will happen? Why do you think so? Then, after reading more, ask: Were you right? How do you know?

Also read some stories *without* asking questions. Let the magic of the story speak for itself.

Read the selections several times so that the children will want to read them for themselves. Older students and parent volunteers can be of great assistance in reading stories and poems to individuals or small groups.

Place books with accompanying records at the reading or listening centre. Children will enjoy using them during the choice period or when other work has been completed.

Visit the local public library as often as possible. Inform the parents of the class visits and of the library activities that would interest their children.

Moving Into Books

Before children are expected to read independently, they should evidence:
1. A love of books.
2. A good concept of reading.
3. An ability to match phrases as they "read" the songs and poems.
4. An ability to match the words.
5. Some strategies for remembering words; that is, they should have a number of sight words.
6. An awareness of rhyme and an ability to make initial consonant substitutions.
7. An ability to predict a word in context when only the initial consonant is given.

Children Who Are Ready

Select a book that relates to the theme and gather together the children whom you feel are ready to read on their own.
1. Talk about the pictures in the book. Ask the children to predict what the story might be about.
2. Read the story to them. Discuss how the characters felt. Have the children share similar experiences which they have had.
3. Have the children read the story on their own. (Do *not* have them read for an audience.) Instruct them to ask for help with words which they do not know. When they ask for help, tell them the word without making any comment about it.
4. At the end of the session, discuss the difficult words. Do not "sound out" the words during the reading since it is important to keep the flow of reading for good comprehension.
5. Reread the story using a variety of techniques such as choral reading or drama.

Children Who Are Reading Fluently

Guide these children by:

1. Supervising their choices of library books.
2. Choosing books of a variety of reading levels relating to the theme for individualized or small group study. It is more important to choose books with relevant subject matter than to choose readers with a controlled vocabulary.
3. Allowing them to read at their level even if they are weak in writing skills. Follow-up activities should include Puppetry, Art, or Drama.
4. Encouraging research activities.

Children Who Are *Not* Ready

It is preferable to have children who are not yet ready to read continue with the poems/songs in *Chime In* than to have them struggle with more advanced reading material. Reading must always be enjoyable. Nothing discourages children more than working with material that is too difficult for them. It is most important to maintain both their interest and their self-confidence.

Therefore, continue to use the poems and songs in *Chime In* as a basis for their reading program. The entire class will enjoy learning the poems/songs, but only those who are not yet ready for books will need to continue making word cards.

Research Activities

Suggestions for research projects are made in this *Guide* (for example, with *Ten Little Squirrels* on p.73). It is advisable to follow the procedure outlined here or a similar procedure with the group as a whole the first time around. The result will be a co-operative booklet. After that, the children who are ready could work on their own.

1. Help the child to choose a topic for research and to list the sub-topics. Encourage the child to choose a sub-topic of particular interest.
2. Allow the child to go to the library or to the reading centre in the classroom. In order to discourage copying of sentences from books, give the child a narrow piece of ruled paper and instruct him or her to print one or two words on each line (see the sample on this page). These constitute the "rough notes" made while locating research material.

Appearance

Red Breast

Black Beak

Model suggested for making rough notes while locating research material.

3. On returning to class, have the child use the rough notes to write a few sentences about the sub-topic. The child should illustrate the sentences as well. The finished product is then stored in the child's individualized *Chime In* book for later access.
4. At the next opportunity to do research, the child chooses another sub-topic and follows the same procedure.
5. When all the sub-topics have been covered, the child arranges them in order, numbers the pages, and makes a Table of Contents.
6. To complete the research project, the child should make and illustrate a cover for the report.

Goals, Activities, and Planning

Each of the activity forms recommended for use in *Chime In* is related to specific developmental goals. The following is a brief summary of these goals:

Activity Form	Goal
Language	To provide daily opportunities for listening, speaking, reading, and writing.
Mathematics	To provide experience in number, measurement, and geometry.
Art	To promote sensory and aesthetic awareness and the development of skills and techniques through various media.
Drama	To provide daily opportunities for expressing feelings, experimenting with ideas, trying out new roles, and interacting in non-threatening situations.
Environmental Studies	To stimulate children to question, explore, and be involved in discovering their world.
Music	To have the children enjoy and experience music through singing, playing, listening, improvising, moving, and dramatizing.
Physical Education	To provide experiences to foster body awareness, movement in space, self-confidence, problem-solving, and physical fitness.

The charts on pages 11 to 14 present for your convenience a complete overview of activities related to the *Chime In* themes and goals. You will see that Language, Mathematics, Art, Environmental Studies, Music, and Physical Education are all categorized as a separate activities. Drama is not so categorized because drama is an integral part of *all* learning for primary students.

These overview charts also suggest an approximate number of weeks for treatment of each theme. Teachers who wish to develop a reading program for the full school year may find these approximations useful as planning guides.

The chart on page 15 suggests a daily timetable that you may find useful as a planning guide.

Chime In Activity Overview

Theme and Date	Language	Mathematics	Art	Environmental Studies	Music	Physical Education
About Me Four Weeks in September	Reading. Puppets and mime. Drama. Alphabet. Parents' stories. Listening to stories. Listen and tell. Discuss. Making books. Printing.	Counting. Measuring. Graphing. Concept of most and fewest. Concept of tall, taller, tallest.	Colouring. Colour charts. Cutting. Pasting. "Me" Quilt. Wall display (Birthday Train). Collage.	My Birthday. My clothes. My colours. Places I go. Safety. My friends. Different styles of writing.	Singing. Singing games. Adding verses. Listening.	Different ways of walking. Outdoor walk. Ropes, shapes of letters. Game (Streets and Roads). Streamers. Parachute activities (different levels).
Harvest and Thanksgiving Two Weeks in October	Reading. Listening to stories. Making books and thank you cards. Following a recipe. Reading menus and newspaper ads. Writing colour verses. Making lists.	Sets. Working with money. Concepts of $\frac{1}{2}$ and $\frac{1}{4}$. Following a recipe. Sequencing.	Mural. Paper tearing. Cutting. Painting. Plasticene modelling.	Our dependence on the farmer. Visit an apple orchard. Visit a supermarket. Recognition of fruit and vegetables. Senses and colours. Thanksgiving.	Singing. Composing new verses. Concept of high and low. Playing instruments.	Concept of high and low. Skipping. Listen and move. Singing game.
Fall and Hallowe'en Two Weeks in October	Reading. Telling and listening to stories. Interviewing a friend. Poetry. Making sentences with word cards. Making Hallowe'en books. Choral speaking.	Counting. Numeral recognition. Sets. Sorting and classifying by shape, colour, and size. Copying designs. Buying a pumpkin.	Wax leaves. Make leaf people. Leaf mobile. Sponge painting. Weaving placemats. Make a design with seeds. Carve a Jack O' Lantern.	Nature hike (tape sounds, collect leaves, seeds, and weeds). Classification of seeds. Visit a market garden. Safety on Hallowe'en.	Experiment with instruments. Listening. Singing. Composing new verses. Make a tape of Hallowe'en sounds.	Creative movement. Relay game. Dramatize songs.

Chime In Activity Overview

Theme and Date	Language	Mathematics	Art	Environmental Studies	Music	Physical Education
Ready for Winter Two Weeks in November	Reading. Listening to stories. Making books about wool. Mitten puppets. Research. Chanting. Drama.	Number facts. Subtraction stories. Matching number word with numeral.	Weaving. Making pictures with paint and material. Making bird feeders.	Story of wool. Comparing fabrics. Visit a pioneer house. Animals preparing for Winter.	Singing. Creating new verses. Listening. Concept of $>$.	Climbing apparatus. Concepts of on/off, under/over, near/far. Winter hike. Game. Relaxation.
Winter Festivities Four Weeks in November and December	Reading. Making commercials. Sorting cards. Story sequence. Listening to stories and poems. Sentence puzzles. Drama. Making charts and books. Writing sentences.	Pricing toys. Measurements in baking. Pathways. Concept of longer and shorter. Following a recipe.	Stick puppets. Felt designs. Christmas decorations. Box sculpture. Painting. Christmas card gingerbread boxes. Make a dreydl.	Favourite toys (sharing and classifying). Discuss sharing. Visit stores. Senses. Special days (a time to show love). Visit a woodlot to buy a tree. Stamp collection.	Create sound effects. Concept of high and low (bells, strings). Chanting. Singing. Listening. Rhythm stories.	Creative movement. Jingle bell folk dance. Pathways. Skipping. Ball bouncing.
Telling Time Two Weeks in January	Reading. Listening to stories. Making wishes. Making books. Writing invitations. Writing stories.	Telling time. Position of sun (big and little shadows).	Crayon resist. Making clocks. Mouse puppet.	Awareness of time Different kinds of clocks. Sun, moon, stars. Shadows. Night walk.	Sounds of clocks. Clapping and chanting. Scale song. Listening.	Shadow walk. Listen and respond (wish and dream). Game. Skipping. Ball bouncing.

Chime In Activity Overview

Theme and Date	Language	Mathematics	Art	Environmental Studies	Music	Physical Education
Winter Two Weeks in January	Reading. Listening to stories. Telling and writing stories. Mime. Writing experiments. Writing new verses.	Reading thermometers. Addition. Shape. Volume (snow and melted snow).	Cutting snowflakes. Making snow scenes with soapflakes and with snow. Mural.	Enjoying winter. Experiments with ice and snow. Using magnifying glass, thermometer. Winter hike.	Singing. Listening Adding sound effects. Creating new verses.	Outdoor play (making snow figures, walking in deep snow). Ways of moving down. Winter hike. Singing game.
Valentines and Mail Two Weeks in February	Reading. Writing Valentines and envelopes. Reading signs and tickets. Listening to stories. Describing.	Weighing. Buying stamps. Pricing tickets. Count by 2's (odd and even).	Mural. Sewing Valentine envelopes. Woodwork.	Valentine's Day. Mailing letters. Visit post office. Transportation (visit airport, train station).	Singing. Concept of fast/slow, faster/slower. Adding sound effects.	Singing games. Slow, slower slowest. Fast, faster, fastest.
Health Two Weeks in February	Reading. Discussion. Listening to stories. Creating new verses. Make a shopping list of good foods. Drama.	Subtraction. Measuring (spoons, cups). Bar graphs. Recognition of nickel, dime, and quarter. Mass. Height.	Sand pictures. Picture charts of good meals.	Keeping healthy and tidy. Dentist. Doctor. Manners.	Singing. Listening. Accompanying.	Singing game. Concept of left and right. Listen and move. Blowing feathers.

Chime In Activity Overview

Theme and Date	Language	Mathematics	Art	Environmental Studies	Music	Physical Education
Weather Two Weeks in March	Reading. Making books. Word families. Listening to stories. Quotation marks. Matching sentences with pictures.	Graph. Perspective (things look smaller far away). Shapes. Measurement. Counting backwards. Sequencing.	Making boats and kites. Illustrating books. Rainbow pictures.	Wind. Rain. Evaporation. Sunshine. Compass. Visit a tall building.	Musical story. Singing. Listening. Accompanying. Adding verses.	Keep balloons in the air. Chanting game. Making shapes with streamers. Outdoor walk.
Spring Four Weeks in March and April	Reading. Calendars. Making Spring books. Listening to stories and poems. Mime. Research. Contractions. Making Easter cards.	Reading a thermometer. Counting by 2's, 5's, and 10's. Placement (units, tens). Shapes. Hopscotch math.	Spring wall-hanging (stitching). Giant worm puppets. Make baskets (folding, cutting, pasting). Colouring eggs. Paper bag birds.	Spring (early signs). Easter. Recognition of birds and flowers. Planting seeds. Microscope. Tadpoles. Gardening.	Singing. Listening. Adding verses. Singing game. Concept of $\leq$ and $\geq$. Accompanying.	Hoop activities. Hopping. Hike (look for signs of Spring). Relay game. Trampoline. Tumbling. Creative movement.
My Family Two Weeks in May	Reading. Listening to stories. Telling stories. Dramatic play. Flannel board stories. Puppets.	Graph. Sets. Addition and subtraction. Numeral words. Counting backwards. Concept of $\frac{1}{2}$, $\frac{1}{4}$, and half dozen.	Finger puppets. Collage. Painting Modelling. Vegetable prints. Make gifts for mother.	Family members (helping and sharing). Safety at home. Pets. Visit pet store and fire station. Mother's Day.	Making rhythm patterns. Singing. Listening. Playing the autoharp. Adding sound effects.	Listen and respond. Relaxation. Skipping. Singing game. Climbing apparatus. Rope activity.
Summer Fun Four Weeks in May and June	Reading. Write a letter. Research. Reply to an invitation. Make a shopping list. Listening to stories. Mime. Question and answer. Making books.	Classification of animals. Shapes. Attribute blocks. Weighing. Balancing.	Frieze of animals in the zoo. Three-dimensionsl shapes. Tissue paper designs. Make animals using stones and pebbles. Illustrating books.	Visit the zoo. Recognition of animals. Safety in the playground and at the beach. Care of toys. Planning a picnic. Magnets.	Improvise sounds to imitate animals. Accompanying. Listening. Singing. Adding verses.	Ropes (make cages of different shapes). Walk like animals. Move on different body parts. Making shapes with body. Singing games.

Chime In Daily Timetable Planning Guide

09:00   Opening Exercises.
        Discussion of Theme.
        Story, Songs, Poetry.

09:30   Physical Education*

10:00   Individual Book Time.

10:10   Introduction of Activities.

10:30   Recess.

10:45   Story, Song, Game.

11:00   Activities**

12:00   Lunch

13:30   Song, Picture Study, Film, Puppet
        Play.

13:45   Activities.**

14:30   Recess.

14:45   Choice Activity.
        Teacher observes children and checks
        completed tasks.*

15:15   Evaluation and Sharing.

   *   May be interchanged.

  **   The class is divided into four groups.
       These may change frequently to
       accommodate the social, emotional,
       and academic needs of the children.
         Plan a two-day cycle. At each
       activity, children are assigned one or
       two tasks. When these are completed,
       they are allowed to choose a game or
       activity at their centre. The chart
       below suggests a possible rotation for
       four groups of children.

	DAY I		DAY II	
	A.M.	P.M.	A.M.	P.M.
Creative Arts	1	2	3	4
Writing	2	3	4	1
Mathematics	3	4	1	2
Reading	4	1	2	3

This program was suggested by Patti Wilson, teacher, North York Board of Education. When routines are firmly established, she finds that she is able to work with groups or individuals during the activity period.

Open Program

Some teachers are more comfortable with a more "open" program. A board displaying pockets labelled with the available activities serves as the organizer of the activity periods. When the children choose an activity, they put their name card in the correct pocket. Students must show their completed task before moving to another activity. The teacher records the completed tasks, noting any specific problems or gains.

Teachers may use these records to plan for small-group or individual instruction or to direct the child's first activity. For example, if the teacher notes that the child has not worked at the math centre, he or she could ensure that the child started with this activity.

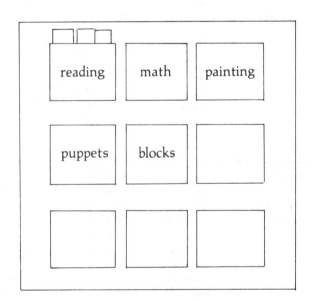

It is most important, whatever the routine, that an activity-oriented environment be established since primary children learn through the manipulation of materials and through play.

Evaluating, Programming, and Reporting

It is crucial for all teachers to develop a system for evaluating and recording individual student progress in order to:
1. Keep tabs on each student's development.
2. Develop special activities to help students experiencing special difficulties or to provide additional challenges.
3. Provide a written record as an aid to memory when preparing reports for the parents and for school records.

The following charts suggest guidelines for observing student progress and developing programs to help students who demonstrate particular needs or talents. These are followed by a suggestion for recording progress as a basis for needed permanent records (pages 18 to 19).

Evaluating and Programming

Social and Emotional Development

Note: If physical, social, or emotional behaviour cannot be modified through the classroom program, seek further assessment without delay. Early identification of problems in these areas is essential for preventing academic difficulties.

Teacher Observation	Suggested Program
Plays well. Appears happy and relaxed.	Extend the learning that is going on during play.
Lacks initiative. Always a follower.	Encourage new friendships. Build self-confidence.
Not free to express feelings.	More play. Encourage creative art activities.

Teacher Observation	Suggested Program
Parallel play rather than involvement with others.	Encourage play close to others.
Lacks consideration of others.	Puppet play. Encourage expression of feelings.
Shows aggression and anger.	Guide play into less frustrating roles. Discuss behaviour and have child label feelings. More creative art activities.

Physical Development

Note: During creative movement and dance activities, the teacher should observe imagination in interpretation; awareness of music; uniqueness of movement; grace of movement; control and use of body parts; posture, stance, and presence; and concentration on the task.

Teacher Observation	Suggested Program
Poor attention span. Difficulty in following directions.	Suggest to parents that the child's hearing be checked.
Awkward or accident-prone. Lack of interest in picture studies and words.	Suggest that the child's vision be tested.
Inability to hold pencil correctly. Poor fine-motor control.	Chalkboard work using complete arm movements. Sand and water play. Modelling with clay or plasticene. Creative dance.

Academic Development

Note: The children will show their readiness for academic development if the activities are open-ended enough to allow them to experiment with new skills.

Reading

Teacher Observation	Suggested Program
Looks at pictures and sings or recites.	Not ready to isolate words. Continue to teach by rote. Have child listen to records or tapes with books.
Notices similar words in songs and poems. Discovers long or short words, words that start like others, etc.	Ready to build sight vocabulary.
Has a large sight vocabulary and enjoys playing with words. Is able to anticipate the correct word in a sentence.	Ready to begin easy books, many of which have been read to him/her first.
Reads easily books which have been previously read to him/her.	Ready to read easy books on his/her own. Note any difficult words. Discuss them after the story.

Writing

Teacher Observation	Suggested Program
Little interest in printing.	Encourage painting, colouring, plasticene modelling, or any other activity to develop fine motor skills. Provide magic markers and large sheets of paper.
Chooses to copy words during activity time.	Ready to begin word cards.
Enjoys copying songs and poems.	Ready to print new verses with minor changes.
Makes new verses without copying word by word.	Ready for more creative writing.

Mathematics

Note: Play activities should provide for concrete experience in number, mass, and measure.

Teacher Observation	Suggested Program
Counts easily and correctly.	Work on sets.
Recognizes numerals.	Matching numerals and sets.
Shows ability to share evenly.	Concepts of addition and subtraction.
Shows ability to organize by colour, shape, or size.	Problem-solving using attribute blocks. Geometric designs.
Compares weights and measurements.	Develop ways of recording observations.
Notices similarities and differences.	Graphing.

Reporting

Most parents are willing and eager supporters of a program or approach that they understand. Most are also more willing and able to co-operate with a teacher with whom they have had contact. Therefore, as a first step, describe your program to the parents, either when first meeting them at school opening or by some other means. Be sure to let them know how they can perform a supportive role. This will be particularly important where families may be newcomers to the community and/or to the country.

When meeting with the parents, emphasize that the best way they can help their children is by reading to them at home. Also stress that the children should initiate conversations about their experiences at school. Parents should take an interest when the child talks about school but should not be asking the child to report on his or her activities.

The goal is to help the children develop the feeling that their accomplishments at school are important for personal satisfaction and are, indeed, personally satisfying. Children must never be made to feel that their goal is to fulfil their parents' expectations.

The next step is to keep a written record for each student. Two simple record-keeping

devices are suggested:

1. Prepare and keep a file folder for each child. Use it to store work samples — one sample each of writing, mathematics, and creative arts for each major theme. These will be useful both for your own review of progress and for showing parents.
2. Prepare an evaluation sheet for each theme. List the children's names and make brief notations under each category as a jog to your memory.

Reporting Progress in Reading

Rather than classifying children as non-readers, report the progress they are making in the strategies listed on page 8. The following shows the type of notation that you may find useful:

Chime In Evaluation Sheet

Theme: _About Me_

Date: _September 10-20_

Teacher Name: _L. Mistow_

School/Class: _Parkview 1C_

Student Name	Reading	Writing	Creative Arts	Mathematics	Choices
Andrews J.	Using Pictures	Name O.K.	Painting all one colour	Counting to 5	Plays well Blocks Sand

Blissymbols with Chime In[1]

Materials are available within the *Chime In* program for non-speaking students who use Blissymbols as their means of communication. The Blissymbol module contains Blissymbol blackline duplicating masters, Blissymbol print-outs to cut and paste into the eight *Chime In* books and instructions for the teacher for incorporating the Blissymbol materials into the *Chime In* program.

An approach to reading similar to that recommended for students learning English as a second langugage can be constructively adopted for students who communicate with Blissymbols, expressing their ideas by pointing to Blissymbols on individualized displays containing a range of symbols, from a few to hundreds. These children have been greatly restricted in their language experiences since they are unable to use speech as their primary means of communication. They have not had the many opportunities afforded speaking children to explore concepts, to play with sounds and words, and to enjoy the rhythm of language. However, most Blissymbol users hear within the normal range and can benefit from being involved in all the *Chime In* activities. Further, the reading programs of speaking students can be enriched through the application of Blissymbols to many activities for the entire class.

Blissymbol users bring to the learning situation many experiences in using graphic symbols; these experiences can be used to advantage in their introduction to the reading of print. Blissymbol users have seen symbols sequenced in left-right direction as their symbol messages were recorded; they have observed similar and different shapes; they have thought about sentences and about organizing their ideas in written form.

Blissymbol users' knowledge concerning the presentation of graphic information cannot compensate, however, for the extensive learning that occurs as young speaking children ask hundreds of questions to find out about their world. *Chime In*, by providing enriching language-related experiences, offers Blissymbol users the opportunity to fill in many experiential gaps. The Blissymbol module provides them with a bridge between their communication system and print.

Blissymbolics[2] is a system used internationally by non-speaking people. Some Blissymbols are pictographs, looking like the things they represent; some are ideographs, portraying a concept through a familiar association; others are simple shapes chosen arbitrarily. The major difference between Blissymbols and print is the manner in which they represent meaning. Blissymbols are composed of shapes, each of which relates *directly* to a meaning. In print, meaning is represented indirectly; the letters relate to sounds which, in combination, form words. There is no clue to meaning until students unlock the sounds of the word and associate the printed word with their knowledge of the spoken word.

Blissymbol activities can be used to help speaking students who are having difficulty relating to words. The symbols give them graphic representations that can be explained according to their meaning parts rather than their letter sounds. The system of Blissymbolics also provides an enrichment experience for students who master print readily and require further learning challenges.

The instructional flexibility offered by Blissymbolics makes an exciting component within the open-ended and integrated approach provided by *Chime In*. For the teacher who is given the opportunity of introducing reading to a Blissymbol user, or who wishes to further expand the *Chime In* program, the Blissymbol module provides many stimulating teaching activities.

[1] Shirley McNaughton, Executive Director, Blissymbolics Communication Institute.

[2] References relating to the system and its use are listed under the heading "Teacher Print Resources" on page 23.

Chime In Resource Lists

Chime In contains 53 poems and songs divided into 13 theme units. This *Guide* contains specific suggestions for other print and non-print resource materials as well. In addition, it is recommended that teachers locate and use other resources available in the school and the community.

As a first step, survey the resources available *before* beginning presentation of the theme. When you conduct your survey, begin with the school library and resource centre. (Your school's librarian will be of great help in gathering materials related to the theme.) Then fan out to public libraries and information centres.

Consider print materials, such as books, picture sets, sheet music, and selections from anthologies. There may be multiple copies of easy-to-read books available in the library, or there may be some single copies of individual titles that could be placed in your classroom reading centre.

Consider non-print materials, such as films, filmstrips, records, and tapes. A filmstrip projector could be set up in the classroom at one of the activity centres, for example, so that the children can view filmstrips invididually or with a partner.

Remember to think in terms of people—colleagues, parents, and others in the community who may have ideas or special skills to offer and who may be willing to visit the class or to assist with out-of-school events. Send a note to the parents telling them of the theme and asking if they have any hobbies or experiences that they could share with the children. Invite others, such as a public health nurse, a police officer, a firefighter, or a camp counsellor, to speak to the class when appropriate to the theme.

Keep a record of resources as you locate them and make notes about their value as you use them. In time, you will build an invaluable record of materials and people particularly well-suited to the needs of your students in the context of the community. To assist you, a record form has been placed at the beginning of each theme unit in this *Guide* (see, for example, pages 26 and 27). You will likely find that this record form or a similar one will answer the need for a record-keeping and evaluating device.

Bibliography

Children's Books

General

Asch, Frank. *Sand Cake*. New York: Parents' Magazine Press, 1979.

Balion, Lorna. *Bah! Humbug?* Nashville: Abingdon Press, 1977.

Barry, Robert. *Mr. Willowby's Christmas*. New York: McGraw-Hill, 1963.

Barrett, Judi. *Benjamin's 365 Birthdays*. New York: Atheneum, 1977.

Beskow, Elsa. *Pelle's New Suit*. New York: Harper and Row, 1929.

Brandenburg, Franz. *No School Today*. New York: Macmillan, 1975.

Bulla, Clyde. *St. Valentine's Day* and *What Makes a Shadow?*. New York: Thomas Y. Crowell, 1962.

Burton, Virginia Lee. *Katy and the Big Snow*. Boston: Houghton-Mifflin, 1943.

Calhoun, Mary. *Euphonia and the Flood*. New York: Parents' Magazine Press, 1976.

Child, Lydia Maria. *Over the River and Through the Wood*. New York: Coward, McCann & Geoghegan, 1974.

Crews, Donald. *Freight Train*. New York: Greenwillow Publishers, 1978.

DeLage, Ida. *The Witchy Broom*. Champaign: Garrard Publishing, 1969.

De Regniers, Beatrice. *May I Bring a Friend*. New York: Atheneum, 1964.

Engelbrektson, Sune. *The Sun is a Star*. New York: Holt, Rinehart & Winston, 1963.

Farber, Norma. *Never Say Ugh! to a Bug*. New York: Greenwillow Publishers, 1979.

Flack, Marjorie. *Angus and the Ducks*. New York: Doubleday, 1930.

Hoban, Russell. *Bedtime for Francis*. New York: Harper and Row, 1960.

Howes, Judy. *What I Like About Toads*. New York: Thomas Y. Crowell, 1969.

Kay, Helen. *An Egg is for Wishing*. New York: Abelard-Schuman, 1966.

Keats, Ezra J. *A Letter to Amy*. New York: Harper and Row, 1968.

Knotts, Howard. *Great-Grandfather, the Baby and Me*. Toronto: McClelland & Stewart, 1978.

Kuskin, Karla. *In the Flaky Frosty Morning*. New York: Harper and Row, 1969.

Littledale, Freya. *The Magic Fish*. Toronto: Scholastic, 1962.

Lobel, Arnold. *The Great Blueness and Other Predicaments*. New York: Harper and Row, 1968.

Martin, Jr., Bill. *Frogs in a Pond* and *June Bugs*, Chicago: Encyclopedia Britannica, 1975.

Martin, Jr., Bill. *Brown Bear, Brown Bear, Fire! Fire! said Mrs. McGuire*, and *A Spooky Story*: Instant Readers. Toronto: Holt, Rinehart & Winston, 1970.

McCloskey, Robert. *Make Way for Ducklings*. New York: Viking Press, 1969.

Milne, A. A. *Now We Are Six*. New York: Dell Publishing, 1979.

Milne, A. A. *Winnie the Pooh and the Honey Tree*. New York: Western Publications, 1976.

Miriam, Eve. "Counting Out Rhymes", *Rainbow Writing*. New York: Atheneum, 1976.

O'Neill, Mary. *Hailstones and Halibut Bones*. New York: Doubleday, 1961.

Palmer, Helen. *I Was Kissed by a Seal at the Zoo*. New York: Beginner Books (Random House), 1962.

Petie, Haris. *The Seed the Squirrel Dropped*. Elizabeth: Prentice-Hall, 1976.

Poulet, Virginia. *Blue Bug's Vegetable Garden*. Chicago: Children's Press, 1973.

Provenson, A. M. *A Peaceable Kingdom*. New York: Viking Press, 1978.

Rey, Margaret. *Curious George Goes to the Hospital*. Boston: Houghton-Mifflin, 1966.

Rey, Margaret. *Curious George Rides a Bike*. Boston: Houghton-Mifflin, 1952.

Sendak, Maurice. *Chicken Soup With Rice*. Toronto: Scholastic, 1962.

Shecter, Ben. *Partouche Plants a Seed*. New York: Harper and Row, 1966.

Skorpen, Liesel. *Old Arthur*. New York: Harper and Row, 1972.

Silverstein, Shel. *The Giving Tree*. New York: Harper and Row, 1964.

Strivastava, Jane Jonas. *Weighing and Balancing*. Toronto: Fitzhenry & Whiteside, 1970.

Tresselt, Alvin. *Hi! Mister Robin*. New York: Lothrop, Lee & Shepard, 1950.

Tresselt, Alvin. *Johnny Maple Leaf*. New York: Lothrop, Lee & Shepard, 1948.

Tresselt, Alvin. *Rain Drop Splash*. New York: Lothrop, Lee & Shepard, 1946.

Tudor, Tasha. *A Tale for Easter*. New York: Henry Z. Wolck, 1973.

Viorst, Judith. *Rosie and Michael*. New York: Atheneum, 1974.

Wabe, Bernard. *You Look Ridiculous Said the Rhinoceros to the Hippopotamus*. Boston: Houghton-Mifflin, 1966.

Ward, Lynd. *The Biggest Bear*. Boston: Houghton-Mifflin, 1952.

Waterton, Betty. *A Salmon for Simon*. Vancouver: Douglas & McIntyre, 1978.

Weiss, Leattie. *Heather's Feathers*. New York: Franklin Watts, 1976.

Weygant, Sister Noemi. *It's Fall* and *It's Winter*. Philadelphia: Westminster Press, 1949.

Zion, Gene. *Harry the Dirty Dog*. New York: Harper and Row, 1956.

Zion, Gene. *The Summer Snowman*. New York: Harper and Row, 1955.

Zolotov, Charlotte. *If It Weren't for You*. New York: Harper and Row, 1966.

Zolotov, Charlotte. *When the Wind Stops*. New York: Harper and Row, 1962.

North American Indian

Baylor, Byrd, and Peter Parnall. *They Put on Masks*. New York: Charles Scribner's Sons, 1974.

Baylor, Byrd, and Peter Parnall. *The Other Way to Listen*. New York: Charles Scribner's Sons, 1978.

Fire Thunder Billy. Toronto: Holt, Rinehart & Winston, 1963.

The Loon's Necklace. Toronto: Oxford University Press, 1977.

Mother Meadowlark and Brother Snake. Toronto: Holt, Rinehart & Winston, 1963.

Eskimo

Field, Edward. *Eskimo Songs and Stories*. New York: Dell Publishing, 1973.

Marsh, Winifred Petchey. *People of the Willow*. Toronto: Oxford University Press, 1976. (The Padlimut tribe is portrayed in watercolours. The original watercolours were presented to Queen Elizabeth II as a Jubilee Year gift.)

Puerto Rico, Alaska, Virgin Islands, Hawaii

Cothran, Jean. *The Magic Calabash*. Madison: Hale and Company, 1965.

France

Francoise. *Noel for Jeanne Marie*. New York: Charles Scribner's Sons, 1974.

Francois, André. *Crocodile Tears*. London: Faber and Faber, n.d. (The text is in English and French.)

China

Abisch, Roz. *Mai-Ling and the Mirror*. Elizabeth: Prentice-Hall, 1969.

Handforth, Thomas. *Mei Li*. New York: Doubleday, 1958.

Hou-tien, Cheng. *The Chinese New Year*. New York: Holt, Rinehart & Winston, 1976.

Africa

Aardema, Verna. *Why Mosquitoes Buzz in People's Ears*. New York: Dial Press, 1975.

Haley, Gail. *A Story — A Story*. New York: Atheneum, 1970.

Musgrove, Margaret. *Ashanti to Zulu*. New York: Dial Press, 1976. (This book offers insights into 26 African tribes.)

India

Bang, Betsy. *The Old Woman and the Rice Thief*. New York: Greenwillow Publishers, 1978.

Duff, Maggie. *Rum, Pum, Pum*. New York: Macmillan, 1978.

U.S.S.R.

Ginsburg, Mirra. *Striding Slippers*. New York: Macmillan, 1978.

Norway

Parin, d'Aulaire. *Ingri and Edgar*. New York: Doubleday, 1933.

Ukraine

Kay, Helen. *An Egg is for Wishing*. New York: Abelard-Schuman, 1966.

Mexico

Dolch, Wedward W., and Marguerite P. Dolch. *Stories from Mexico*. Champaign: Garrard Publishing, 1960.

Jewish

Aleichem, Sholem. *Hanukkah Money*. New York: Greenwillow Publishers, 1978.

Simon, Norma. *Hanukkah*. New York: Thomas Y. Crowell, 1966.

Children's Records

Anderson, ____ . *The Syncopated Clock.*
Bach, J.S. "Badinerie" and "Polonaise", *Orchestral Suite #2.*
Beethoven, Ludwig von. *Albumblatt.*
Brahms, Johannes. *Lullaby.*
Debussy, Claude. "The Snow is Dancing", *Children's Corner Suite.*
Delibes, Leo. "Pizzicato", *Sylvia Ballet.*
Disney, Walt. "Spoonful of Sugar", *Mary Poppins.*
Grieg, Edward, "In the Hall of the Mountain King", *Peer Gynt Suite.*
Hardie, Marilyn, and Elaine Mason. *Music Builders, No. 1.* (Berandol.)
Humperdinck, Engelbert. "Children's Prayer", *Hansel and Gretel.*
MacDowell, Edward. "March Winds", *Twelve Virtuoso Studies*, Opus 46.
MacDowall, Edward. "Shadow Dance", *2nd Modern Suite*, Opus 14.
Maxwell and Sigman. *Ebb Tide.*
Mendelssohn, Felix. *Voices of Spring.*
Palmer, Hap. "Sea Gulls" and "Getting to Know Myself", *Learning Basic Skills Through Music.* (Educational Activities, Inc.)
Saint-Saëns, Camille. *Le Carnaval des Animaux.*
Schumann, Robert. "The Happy Farmer", *Album for the Young.*
Tchaikovsky, Peter. *The Nutcracker Suite* and *Serenade for String Orchestra in C Major*, Opus 48.
Rodgers and Hammerstein. "My Favourite Things", *The Sound of Music.*

Teacher Print Resources

Baratta-Lorton, Mary. *Mathematics Their Way.* Don Mills: Addison-Wesley, Publishing Co., 1976
Bliss, Charles K. *Semantography.* Sydney: Semantography Publications, 1965.
Blissymbolics Communication Institute. *Independent Study Program.* Toronto: Blissymbolics Communication Institute, 1985.
Boorman, Joyce. *Dance and Language Experiences with Children.* Toronto, Longman, 1973.
Donaldson, Margaret. *Children's Minds.* New York: W.W. Norton and Company, 1978.
Graves, Donald H. *Writing: Teachers and Children at Work.* New Hampshire: Heinemann Educational Books, 1983.
Hamlin, Alice P., and Margaret G. Guessford. *Singing Games for Children.* Cincinnati: Willis Music Co., 1941.

Hehner, Barbara. *Blissymbols for Use.* Toronto: Blissymbolics Communication Institute, 1980.
Helfman, Elizabeth. *Blissymbolics: Speaking Without Speech.* New York: Elsevier/Nelson Books, 1981.
Holdaway, Donald. *The Foundations of Literacy.* Toronto: Ashton Scholastic, 1979.
Huck, Charlotte. *Children's Literature in the Elementary School.* New York: Holt, Rinehart and Winston, 1979.
McDonald, Eugene. *Teaching and Using Blissymbolics.* Toronto: Blissymbolics Communication Institute, 1980.
McNaughton, Shirley (ed.) *Communicating with Blissymbolics.* Toronto: Blissymbolics Communication Institute, 1985.
Meek, Margaret. *Learning to Read.* London: The Bodley Head, 1982.
Mursell, James L., et al. *Music for Living Through the Day.* Morristown: Silver Burdett, 1960.
Rosenblatt, Louise. *The Reader, the Text, and the Poem.* Carbondale, Ill.: Southern Illinois University Press, 1978.
Sharp, Evelyn. *Thinking is Child's Play.* New York: E.P. Dutton, 1969.
Singer, H., and R. Riddell (ed.). *Theoretical Models and Processes of Reading.* Newark, Delaware: International Reading Association, 1976.
Smith, Frank. *Reading Without Nonsense.* New York: New York Teachers' College Press, 1979.
Smith, Frank. *Understanding Reading: a Psycholinguistic Analysis of Reading and Learning to Read.* Toronto: Holt, Rinehart & Winston, 1971.
Temple, C., R. Nathan, and H. Burris. *The Beginnings of Writing.* Toronto: Allyn & Bacon Inc., 1982.
Tough, Joan. *Focus on Meaning.* London: Allen and Unwin, 1973.
Trealease, Jim. *The Read Aloud Handbook.* Harmondsworth: Penquin, 1982.
Wells, Gordon. *Learning Through Interaction.* Cambridge: Cambridge University Press, 1982.
Wengrov, Rabbi Charles. *Hanukkah in Song and Story.* New York: Shulsinger Brothers Press, 1960.
Western Education Development Group. *Parachutes.* Vancouver: University of British Columbia, n.d.
Williams, E.M., and Hilary Sherard. *Primary Mathematics Today*, New Metric Edition. Toronto: Longman, 1976.
Yardley, Alice. *Young Children Thinking.* London: Evans, 1973.

Theme Unit 1
About Me

About Me Resource Record

Resources Available	*Comments*
Books and Other Print Materials	
Films, Filmstrips, and Other Non-print Materials	

Resources Available	Comments
Records and Tapes	
People in the Community	
Other (Including Equipment)	

Walk to School

Walk, walk, walk to school.
Walk to school together.
Walk, walk, walk to school.
Walk to school together.

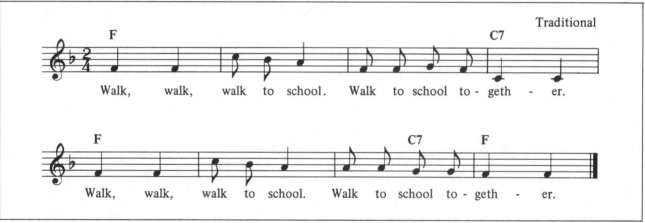

Chime In

1. Teach the song with actions during the physical education period.
2. Have the children suggest other verses.
3. Introduce the wall chart.
4. Sing with the chart.
5. Give each child a copy of the song. (It is recommended that the songs be run off on a standard size sheet punched for a three-ring binder.)

Read

Rosie and Michael, Judith Viorst (Atheneum).

Discuss

1. What do you like to do with your friend?
2. How can you help your friend?

Write

1. Have the children make a title page for their individualized *Chime In* About Me theme books. (The first page of the book will be their copy of the *Walk to School* song.) The title page should include a drawing of themselves.
2. Encourage the children to add another verse to the song to add to their books. (These could be based on actions such as skipping, jumping, hopping, etc.). They may illustrate the new verse with a picture they have drawn or cut from a magazine.

Physical Education

Introduce the concepts of listening and moving:
1. Walk forward, backward, sideways.
2. Find different ways of walking, jumping, hopping.
3. Walk by balancing on different parts of the feet.
4. Play the *Badinerie, Suite #2*, J. S. Bach. Direct the children to move to the music and to use all the available space. Instruct them to change direction when they hear the triangle.

5. Play the *Polonaise, Suite #2*, J. S. Bach. The children should move to the music, use all available space, but bow to a friend when they hear the triangle.

Creative Arts

1. "Let your crayon do the walking." How many different ways can you move your crayon? (Examples are sideways, on the dull end, on the pointed end, lightly, heavily, using two crayons.)

Mathematics

1. Play games involving counting, such as counting steps while walking.
2. Listen to records and tapes of counting rhymes.

Picture Study

1. Show a picture of a child or children going somewhere. Discuss. (Where are they going? Why? What will they do when they get there? How do they feel?)
2. Mount a number of pictures in the language centre. Have students work in pairs. Each should take turns telling a story about a picture.

Stop! Look! Listen!

Stop!
Look!
Listen!
Before you cross the street.
Use your eyes.
Use your ears.
Then use your feet.

6

7

Chime In

1. Teach the poem with actions.
2. Present the wall chart.
3. Read the poem together.
4. Add new verses (such as "Before you chase a ball").
5. If you wish, recite the verse with the class every day before dismissal.

Go for a Walk

1. Take the class for a walk with a safety patroller. Look for stop signs and traffic signals.

Read

Make Way for Ducklings, Robert McClosky (Viking Press).

Write

1. Keep wall charts on display near the writing centre.
2. Provide large pieces of newsprint and coloured markers to encourage beginning printers.

Physical Education

1. Play Streets and Roads tag.
   (A) Have the children stand in rows.
   (B) Choose one child to be "it" and another to give chase.
   (C) Instruct the children to join hands across the rows vertically when you call out "street" and to join hands across the rows horizontally when you call out "road".

ROADS

Drama

1. Place a police officer's hat and equipment for safety patrollers in the play centre.
2. Provide large play blocks for building a police station.

Creative Arts

1. Make road signs, traffic signals, and police officer badges. These may be used in conjunction with activities in the drama centre.

Mathematics

1. Introduce the concept of most and fewest:
   (A) Form the children into a circle.
   (B) Place several children holding "No Parking" signs on the perimeter.
   (C) Place one child as police officer in the centre.
   (D) Play music that can be started and stopped with ease. The children walk in a circle until the music stops. Anyone caught beside a "No Parking" sign is given a ticket.
   (E) At the end of the game, count the tickets. Who has the most? Who has the fewest?

The End

When I was One,
I had just begun.
When I was Two,
I was nearly new.
When I was Three,
I was hardly Me.
When I was Four,
I was not much more.
When I was Five,
I was just alive.
But now I am Six,
I'm as clever as clever.
So I think I'll be Six now
Forever and ever.

Chime In

1. Have parents write a short story (one or two paragraphs) about their children's younger days. Read them to the class.
2. Ask the children to show how tall they were at different ages.
3. Recite the poem several times, using variations such as:
   (A) Have the children "fill in the blanks" by calling out the numeral words.
   (B) Have them hold up the correct number of fingers to indicate the age reached.
   (C) Have them "grow" as you recite by rising from a sitting position.
   They will very quickly be reciting the poem with you.
4. Present the wall chart and have the children read it with you.
5. Distribute copies of the poem.

Read

"Counting Out Rhymes", *Rainbow Writing*, Eve Miriam (Atheneum).

Write

1. Have the children make books to illustrate the poem, consisting of one page per year of their ages. Each page should be marked with the relevant age. Have the children draw pictures showing something they liked to do at that age.

Express Feelings

1. Hold up a number card and ask the children to state the number. Hold up the card again, and ask the children to say the number as if they were sad, happy, angry, and frightened.

Physical Education

1. Have the children show how tall they are now and how tall they were at age one, two, etc.
2. Have them move their bodies at different levels:
   (A) Provide small and large equipment to be used at different levels.
   (B) Do parachute activities at different levels.

Mime

1. Have children mime something that they can do.
   (A) Have the other children guess what is being mimed.
   (B) Have the children copy the mimed action.

Invite

1. Ask a mother to demonstrate bathing a baby. (This activity will help prepare children for the arrival of a new baby in their home.)

Drama

1. Provide different sizes of dolls and clothes in the play area. Ask a volunteer to make similar outfits for three sizes of dolls. (This will increase the problem-solving and development of mathematical skills.)

Creative Arts

1. Make an About Me wall hanging using a large sheet of heavy cotton or burlap and felt circles.
   (A) Give each child a felt circle and have him or her make a "portrait" by gluing scraps of wool, fabric, etc., on the circle.
   (B) The "portraits" should then be glued on to the sheet of cotton or burlap.
   (C) The teacher or parent volunteer should then add dowling and edging.
   (D) Use the wall hanging as a divider for the activity centres.

Mathematics

1. Use gummed squares or crayons to make a graph of the poem.

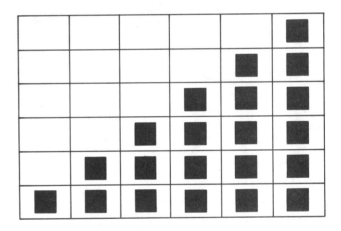

The Alphabet Song

Aa Bb Cc Dd
Ee Ff Gg
Hh Ii Jj Kk
Ll Mm Nn Oo Pp
Qq Rr Ss
Tt Uu Vv
Ww Xx
Yy Zz
Now I've sung my A B C's.
Next time won't you sing with me?

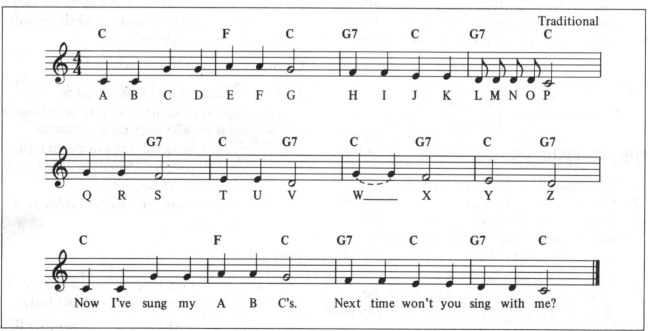

Chime In

1. Point to each letter as you sing or chant.
2. Sing it again without pointing to the letters. Stop singing in the middle of the song, and ask a child to point to the letter at which you stopped.
3. Leave the wall chart in a prominent place so that the children may use it during activity time.

Read

A Peaceable Kingdom, A. M. Provenson (Viking).

Language Centre

1. Provide records and tapes of alphabet songs.
2. Provide a variety of alphabet books.

Write

1. Display sand paper, magnetic, and felt letters.
2. Provide laminated printing cards for tracing. Class names are ideal. Use dots and arrows to show directionality. Use a cursive printing (one continuous stroke).

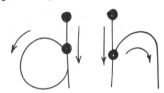

Physical Education

1. Use ropes to make shapes of letters.
2. Play the Musical Letters game. Place large letters on the floor (one fewer than the number of children). When the music stops, each child picks up and names a letter. One child cannot and is declared "out". Remove another letter from the floor, and continue the game until only one child is left.

Wonder Table

1. Display samples of different ways of printing letters (such as Roman, Cyrillic, Arabic, Hebrew, Chinese, Cree, and Algonkian).

Creative Arts

1. Have the children print a letter and then make a path to another. Instruct them to use different colours for each letter. Display the designs.

Mathematics

1. Play the Letter Card game.
   (A) Make several sets of letter cards (one letter per card).
   (B) Assign the children to groups of three.
   (C) One child picks a card. The other two must then find all the cards printed with the same letter.
   (D) Count the letter cards. Who found the most? How many are there altogether?
   (E) Jumble the cards and re-start the game with a different member of the group making the draw.

Game

1. Play the Uppers and Lowers game.
   (A) Give some children capital letter cards and others lower case letter cards.
   (B) At a given signal, they begin to look for their partner. When they find each other, they sit down.
   (C) After naming the letters, jumble and play again.

Story Telling

Tell this story to help emphasize the shapes of letters. Hold up letter cards to demonstrate.

Once upon a time, there was a big brother B. Little b liked her brother so much that she tried to look exactly like him. So she stuck out her tummy in the very same way.

But little d wanted to be different from his big sister D. So little d turned around and stuck out his tummy the other way!

Chime In

1. Introduce the wall chart.
2. Ask the children if they can guess what song it is.
3. Sing with the chart.
4. Have the children take turns holding their name card over the blank in the song.
5. Distribute copies of the song.

Read

Benjamin's 365 Birthdays, Judi Barrett (Atheneum).

Happy Chart

1. Prepare a chart headed, I'm Happy When. . . .
   (A) Ask each child to complete the sentence. Print in the dictated responses.
   (B) Have children sign their names beside their sentences.

Write

1. Have the children print their names in the space on their individualized *Chime In* song sheets. Have them add candles to represent their age.
2. Have the children make name cards to be used as you sing the song with them. Many children have been taught to print only with capital letters. Children who are having difficulty with forming lower case letters should be encouraged to continue tracing. Be sure that children are holding pencils or markers correctly.

Encourage Reading

Encourage the children to take their *Chime In* books to the reading centre. They will enjoy reading with a friend. Reading will be different for each child. Some will just look at the picture and know the song. Others will recognize a few words and others will be following the print perfectly. Everyone will feel successful.

Bake a Cake

1. Tape the sounds involved in baking a cake.
   (A) Get a bowl and spoon.
   (B) Sift the flour.
   (C) Pour milk.
   (D) Crack an egg.
   (E) Beat the batter.
   (F) Pour the batter into the pan.
   (G) Close the oven door.
2. Play the tape of the sounds while telling the cake-baking story.

Drama

1. Place birthday hats, wrapping paper, and tape in the the play area.
2. Have the children choose articles in the classroom and wrap them as presents. The others will guess the contents.

Creative Arts

1. Make a birthday train (one car per month). Have the children print their names or put a photograph behind a window in the correct car.
2. Give children large pieces of paper (of different shapes) to represent cakes. Have them decorate their cakes with crayon or paint.

Mathematics

1. Ask individual children: How old are you? The child should tap on a table or play an instrument to show how old he or she is. The other children should count the taps.
2. Ask other children different questions, such as: How old is the person in the picture? Have them tap out the answers.

Blue Jeans

Cathy wears blue jeans,
Blue jeans, blue jeans.
Cathy wears blue jeans
All day long.

14

15

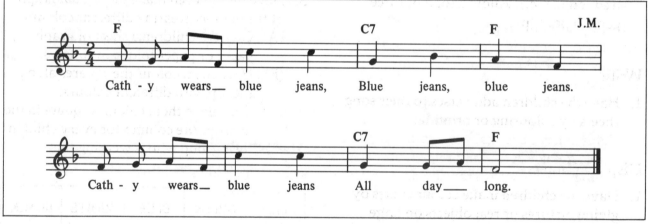

J.M.

Cath - y wears___ blue jeans, Blue jeans, blue jeans.

Cath - y wears___ blue jeans All day___ long.

Chime In

1. Teach the song.
2. Add verses by changing the name, colour, and article of clothing.
3. Play a singing game. The class sings such verses as: Are you wearing a red shirt? Those who are go into the centre of circle and walk to the music.
4. Introduce the wall chart. Sing the song, pointing to the line matching the one you are singing.
5. Distribute copies of the song.

Read

Brown Bear, Brown Bear Instant Reader, Bill Martin, Jr. (Holt, Rinehart & Winston).

The I Spy Game

1. Play the I Spy With My Little Eye game using colours of objects in the room. Each child takes a turn saying: I spy with my little eye something that is __________ (red, blue, etc.). Allow a total of three guesses per I spy.

Write

1. Have the children add verses to their song sheets by colouring or printing.

Display Charts

1. Have the children make colour charts by gluing pictures or real objects on large cards.

Physical Education

1. Play *Serenade for String Orchestra in C Major, Opus 48* (second movement), Peter Tchaikovsky.
   (A) Cut different coloured streamers from crepe paper.
   (B) Direct the children to move to the music, using the streamers to make beautiful designs.
   (C) Encourage them to use all the space and to move on different levels.

Wonder Table

1. Place a selection of paint chips (from a paint store) on the table. Encourage the children to sort the chips into colour groupings. They will learn many more colour words.

Creative Arts

1. Have the children make a collage by cutting out pictures of clothing from magazines. They may also use fabric scraps to make the collage.

Mathematics

1. Make a graph by having the children put a star under their favourite colour.
2. Count the number of children wearing red, blue, green, etc.
3. Have the children make individual graphs of the number wearing different colours.
   (A) Give the children a sheet of graph paper or paper folded in squares.
   (B) Have them colour the squares along the top with different colours.
   (C) Then have them colour a square in the appropriate column for every child in their group who is wearing that colour.

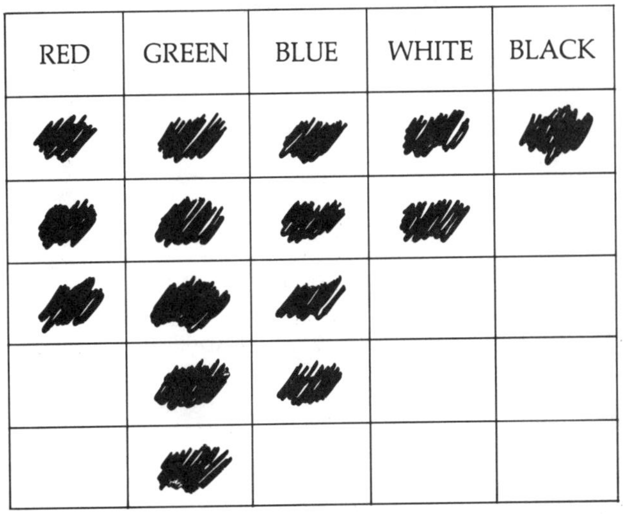
RED
GREEN
BLUE
WHITE
BLACK

Theme Unit 2
Harvest and Thanksgiving

Harvest and Thanksgiving Resource Record

Resources Available	Comments
Books and Other Print Materials	
Films, Filmstrips, and Other Non-print Materials	

Resources Available	*Comments*
Records and Tapes	
People in the Community	
Other (Including Equipment)	

Red, Red

Red, red
What is red?
Apples are red,
Tasty as can be.

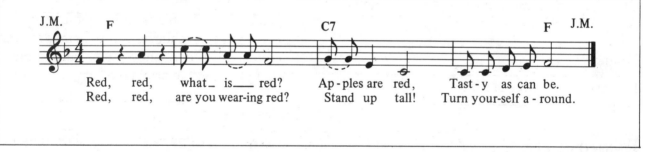

J.M.   F   C7   F   J.M.

Red,   red,   what_ is__ red?   Ap-ples are red,   Tast-y as can be.
Red,   red,   are you wear-ing red?   Stand up   tall!   Turn your-self a-round.

Chime In

1. Teach the song.
2. Discuss the word *tasty*.
3. What else is tasty?
4. Introduce the wall chart.
5. Sing with the wall chart.
6. Ask a child to find the word *red*, *apples*, etc.
7. Distribute copies of the song.
8. Encourage the children to create new verses. Print them on chart paper and add them to the display charts (see *Blue Jeans*, p. 39). An example of a new verse is:

Red, red

Are you wearing red?

Stand up tall!

Turn yourself around.

Read

Hailstones and Halibut Bones, Mary O'Neil (Doubleday).
The Great Blueness and Other Predicaments, Arnold Lobel (Harper and Row).

Display

1. Display pictures of farms, orchards, good food, etc.

Write

1. Have the children make a title page for their individualized *Chime In* Harvest and Thanksgiving theme books.
2. The children may add more verses in their books. Some may be ready to print. Others will be colouring.

Visit

1. Arrange a class visit to an apple orchard, market garden, or farm if possible. Also, buy some apples if possible.

Watch

Show the film *Hailstones and Halibut Bones*, *Part 1* and *Part 2* (National Broadcasting).

Physical Education

1. Using a xylophone, have the children find low, medium, and high sounds. When they hear a low pitch tone, have the children pretend to pick an apple from the ground. A medium pitch is a signal to pick from a low branch, and a high pitch is a signal to pick from a high branch.
2. Vary the speed of the musical tones.

Wonder Table

Have the children bring a variety of fruits and vegetables for display.
1. Play the Touch, Smell, and Taste game. Blindfold a child and have him or her guess which food is selected for a touch, smell, or taste test.
2. Have the children close their eyes. Remove one vegetable or fruit from the display. Which is missing?
3. Put four or five fruits and vegetables in a row. Have the children close their eyes, and change the order. Choose one child to put them back in the original order.

Creative Arts

1. Make a mural by having the children make trees by paper tearing. Add cutouts of ladders and baskets of fruit. Cut out apple shapes and pin them on the trees.
2. Have the children paint pictures of themselves, cut them out, and paste them on the mural.

Mathematics

Follow a recipe to make apple sauce.
1. Print the recipe on a wall chart. Ask a parent volunteer to make apple sauce with small groups.
2. Leave measuring cups and spoons in the sand table so that children can make "pretend apple sauce" during activity time.

If I Were a Farmer

Oh, if I were a farmer,
A farmer, a farmer,
Oh, if I were a farmer
What would I grow?

Some lettuce and carrots
Some green beans and cabbage
Oh, if I were a farmer
That's what I'd grow.

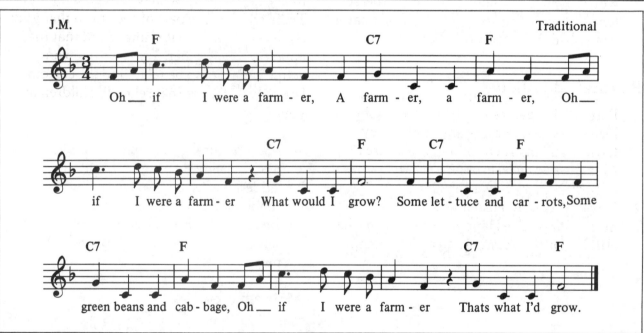

Did you ever see a lassie?

Chime In

1. Teach the song.
2. Use the vegetables and fruits from the wonder table (developed for *Red, Red*, see p. 45) to illustrate the song.
3. Introduce the wall chart.
4. Sing with the wall chart.
5. Ask the children to name other things the farmer could grow. Make a word card for each.
6. Pin these word cards onto the wall chart, and sing the new version of the song.

Read

Blue Bug's Vegetable Garden, Virginia Poulet (Children's Press).

Write

1. The children may draw pictures of things they would grow.
2. Have the children who are ready copy I would grow . . . and then finish the sentence by copying some of the word cards developed as variations of the song.

Physical Education

1. Play singing games — The Farmer in the Dell and Oats, Peas, Beans, and Barley Grow. (Full instructions and music are in *Music for Living Through the Day*, James L. Mursell *et al*, Silver Burdett.)
2. Have the children listen and move to music. Play "The Happy Farmer" from the *Album for the Young*, Robert Schumann.

Creative Arts

1. Make a mural of a fruit and vegetable stand.
   (A) Have the children stuff various-sized bags with torn newsprint and then paint them to represent fruits and vegetables.
   (B) Pin these on the mural.
   (C) Add real cornstalks and a full-sized scarecrow.

Mathematics

1. Price vegetables and fruits by checking newspaper ads or visiting a market garden. Make price signs and pin them on the mural.

Other Harvest Festivals

Primary children are not yet ready to study customs of other lands. However, if you have New Canadians in your class, take the opportunity to discuss how they celebrate harvest. These children are part of the world that your class knows, and so it is important that they appreciate each other. Try to develop an activity that could be related to the custom. Use only resources that relate to children in your class.

Thank You

Thank you, thank you
Let's all sing.
Thank you, thank you
For everything.
Thanks for the flowers,
Thanks for the trees,
Thanks for the sun
That shines on me.
Thank you, thank you
Let's all sing.
Thank you, thank you
For everything.

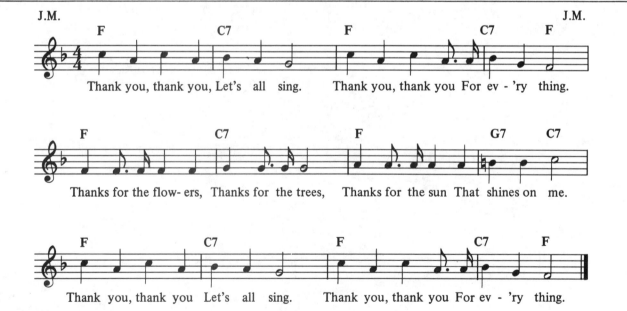

Chime In

1. Discuss things for which we are thankful.
2. Teach the song.
3. Introduce the wall chart.
4. Sing with the wall chart.
5. Sing it again, changing verses by making substitutes for flowers, trees, etc.
6. Match sentences and words as you sing.
7. Distribute copies of the song.

Discuss

1. People for whom we are thankful.
2. Are other people thankful for us?
3. How can we make others happy?

Read

The Giving Tree, Shel Silverstein (Harper and Row).
Over the River and Through the Wood, Lydia Maria Child (Coward, McCann & Geoghegan).

Listen

Play "My Favourite Things" from *The Sound of Music*.

Write

1. Make thank you booklets either individually or co-operatively.
2. Make thank you cards.

Going to the Store

I am going to the store,
To the store, to the store.
I am going to the store.
What do I need?

I need some milk and butter,
Milk and butter, milk and butter.
I need some milk and butter.
That's what I need.

10

11

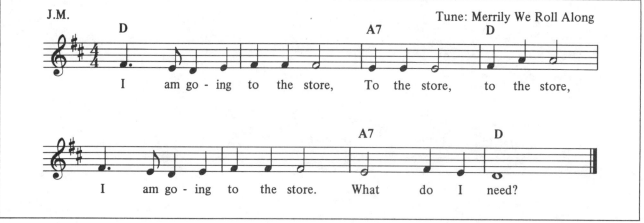

J.M.   Tune: Merrily We Roll Along

Chime In

1. Teach the song.
2. Dramatize with articles from the store (see Drama activity).
3. Introduce the wall chart.
4. Distribute copies of the song.
5. Have the children make more verses by copying from newspaper ads.

Drama

1. Set up a store with empty boxes, cans, a toy cash register, toy money, etc.
2. Shape plasticene meat patties, place them on foam or cardboard trays, and wrap them with plastic.
3. Price the articles.

Write

1. Have one child make up a shopping list by copying from the items for sale in the store.
2. Give the list and a large bag to another child. Can he or she find the correct articles?

Theme Unit 3
Fall and Hallowe'en

Fall and Hallowe'en Resource Record

Resources Available	Comments
Books and Other Print Materials	
Films, Filmstrips, and Other Non-print Materials	

Resources Available	Comments
Records and Tapes	
People in the Community	
Other (Including Equipment)	

The Leaves Are Falling

Down, down, down, down,
The leaves are falling down
In their lovely dresses
Of red and brown.

Down, down, down, down,
While the flowers sleep.
Careful as you run along.
Don't make a peep!

12   13

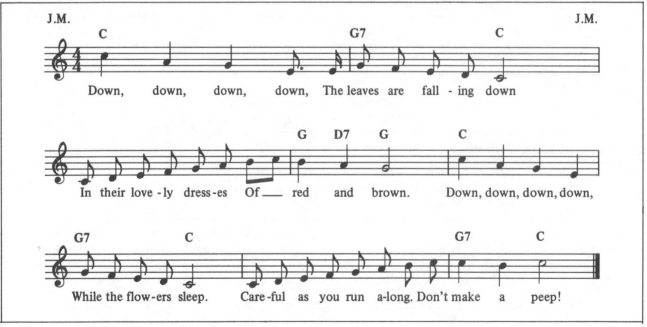

Chime In

1. Teach the song with actions.
2. Introduce the wall chart.
3. Pin other colour words over red and brown, then sing again.
4. Choose some children to be leaves, some to be flowers, others to be the children. Sing again as these children mime the song.
5. Distribute copies of the song.

Read

Johnny Maple Leaf, Alvin Tresselt (Lothrop, Lee & Shepard).

Write

1. Have the children make a title page for their individualized *Chime In* Fall and Hallowe'en theme books.
2. Have them arrange word cards from the song into sentences. Copy their sentences.

Physical Education

1. Play a piece of music such as *Albumblatt* by Ludwig von Beethoven. Have the children imagine what they can hear in the music (for example, a leaf blowing, children running, the wind blowing). Encourage the children to use all the space and to move at different levels. As they move, make suggestions by using words such as spin, twirl, twist, tremble, quiver, soar, fly, sink.

Nature Walk

1. Take the class for a walk in a nearby park or field.
   (A) Collect leaves, seeds, and weeds, and look at colours.
   (B) Break a dead branch and a live branch.
   (C) Tape sounds as you walk.
2. Play the tape, and tell the nature walk story.

Wonder Table

1. Compare live leaves and dry leaves by observation, touch, and mass. (Weigh the leaves.)
2. Arrange a bouquet of weeds and dried flowers.

Creative Arts

1. Make leaf people and animals.
   (A) Iron leaves between two sheets of waxed paper.
   (B) Use the leaf as the body, and add faces and features with scraps of felt, yarn, and fabric.

2. Remove the apples from the *Red, Red* mural (see p. 45). Change the mural by sponge painting with Fall colours to represent leaves on the trees and on the ground.

Mathematics

1. Cut out a large felt tree and place it on a flannel board. Have the children work in pairs. One chooses a number and the other places that number of leaves on the tree.

Rake the Leaves

Here we come to rake the leaves,
Rake the leaves, rake the leaves.
Here we come to rake the leaves.
And make a great big pile.

14

15

J.M.   Tune: Mulberry Bush

Here   we come   to rake   the leaves,   Rake   the leaves,   rake   the leaves.

Here   we come   to rake   the leaves.   And make   a   great   big   pile.

Chime In

1. Teach the song using actions.
2. Introduce the wall chart.
3. Distribute copies of the song.
4. Encourage the children to create new verses.
5. Mount the new verses on the wall chart.

Listening Centre

1. Tape the children singing the song from their *Chime In* books.
2. Leave the tape set up so that the children may bring their books and sing along.

Read

It's Fall, Sister Noemi Weygant (Westminster Press).

Write

1. Have the children add more verses in their individualized *Chime In* books.
2. Make word cards for the new verses.
3. Have children interview a friend and then print or draw a picture of what the friend did on a Fall day.

Physical Education

1. Allow children to experiment with musical instruments to show movements of the leaves. Have the other children imitate the movements of the leaves as one child plays.
2. Play the Relay game. Each child is given a leaf, runs in turn to the basket, deposits the leaf, and runs back to touch the next person, who then takes a turn.

Wonder Table

1. Sort and classify seeds that fly, seeds that animals eat, seeds that stick, and seeds that people eat.

Creative Arts

1. Have the children make leaf mobiles by gluing some pressed leaves on a string and tying them to branches.

Mathematics

1. Continue using the flannel board. Have the children make matching sets of leaves.

Lappy Lappy

a   a   a   a
lappy   lappy   lappy   la
e   e   e   e
leppy   leppy   leppy   le
i   i   i   i
lippy   lippy   lippy   li
o   o   o   o
loppy   loppy   loppy   lo
u   u   u   u
luppy   luppy   luppy   lu
a   e   i   o   u   GRU!

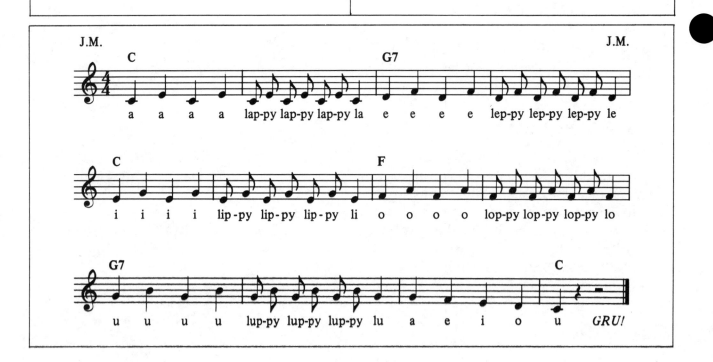

Chime In

1. Teach the song. Do not over-emphasize the vowels. The children will imitate your voice. Encourage them to shape their mouths correctly.
2. Introduce the wall chart and sing with it.
3. Make individual consonant cards. Cover the "l" with another consonant as you sing.
4. Children seem to find this song very satisfying. They love to repeat it. You may wish to place the wall chart in an activity centre for individual use.

Substitute

1. Later in the year, you may make consonant substitutes, such as "dd", "tt", "mm", "ff", and so on, in place of "pp". You may also wish to change the final "-y" to "-le" or "-ing".

4

On Hallowe'en

When I go out on Hallowe'en,
Hallowe'en, Hallowe'en,
When I go out on Hallowe'en
What will I be?

I will be a clown.
I will be a clown.
I will be a clown.
Ha, ha, ha!

5

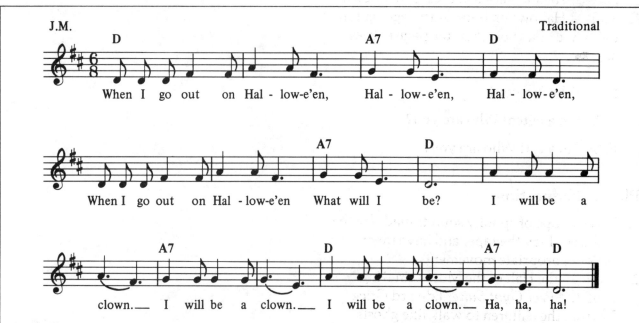

J.M.   Traditional

When I go out on Hal - low-e'en,   Hal - low-e'en,   Hal - low-e'en,

When I go out on Hal - low-e'en   What will I   be?   I   will be   a

clown.__ I will be a clown.__ I will be a clown.__ Ha, ha, ha!

Chime In

1. Teach the song, dramatizing the answer.
2. Introduce the wall chart and sing with it.
3. Have children make new answers to What will I be? Prepare sentence cards of the new answers.
4. Make sentence cards for alternate endings (Ha, Ha, Ha and Oo, Oo, Oo). Let the children decide which ending is appropriate for the new answers. (*Note*: If the Oo, Oo, Oo ending is used while singing, change the D chord to D minor.)

Read

A Spooky Story Instant Reader, Bill Martin, Jr. (Holt, Rinehart & Winston).

Write

1. Have a child write an answer to the What will I be? question on a strip of bristol board.
2. Have them add verses in their own books.
3. Make a Hallowe'en book with pages cut in the shape of a ghost. Sample page entries are:

   P. 1: Who are you?

   P. 2: I'm a witch! Who are you?

   P. 3: I'm a cat! Who are you?

Physical Education

1. Make a tape of spooky sounds made by the children. Play the tape, and have them make appropriate movements.
2. Play "In the Hall of the Mountain King" from the *Peer Gynt Suite*, Edward Grieg. Instruct the children to walk like ghosts, pirates, or witches to the music. At the sound of the cymbal, they should change to another movement.

Visit

1. Visit a market and buy a pumpkin.
2. Carve a Jack O' Lantern.
3. Toast the pumpkin seeds.

Creative Arts

1. Have the children make a wall hanging using pumpkin seeds, milkweed pods, and dried grasses which have been arranged and glued on coloured burlap.

Mathematics

1. Pretend that attribute blocks are candy. Sort them for colour or shape.
2. Have one child make a design with the blocks for another to copy.

Witch, Witch

Witch, witch, where do you fly?
Under the clouds and over the sky.

Witch, witch, what do you eat?
Little black apples from Hurricane Street.

Witch, witch, where do you sleep?
Up in the clouds, where pillows are cheap.

6

7

Chime In

1. Teach the poem.
2. Instruct one group of students to take the ghost role and ask questions with you. The other group should take the witch role and answer with you.
3. Ask students how would they speak their roles if the witch were deaf, if they didn't want anyone else to hear, or if they were frightened.
4. Think of as many ways as possible to recite the poem.
5. Distribute song sheets.

Read

The Witchy Broom, Ida DeLage (Garrard Publishing).
They Put on Masks, Byrd Baylor (Charles Scribner's).

Discuss

1. Safety on Hallowe'en night.

Write

1. Cut a large pumpkin out of construction paper. Have the children print Hallowe'en words on it.

Drama

1. Place several Hallowe'en costumes in the play centre.

Creative Arts

1. Weave placemats with strips of orange and black paper.

Story Telling

1. Place Hallowe'en pictures at the listening centre. Have a child tell a story, and tape it.
2. If you plan a class Hallowe'en party, the taped stories could be played as part of the entertainment.

Theme Unit 4
Ready for Winter

Ready for Winter Resource Record

Resources Available	Comments
Books and Other Print Materials	
Films, Filmstrips, and Other Non-print Materials	

	Resources Available	Comments
Records and Tapes		
People in the Community		
Other (Including Equipment)		

Baa, Baa Black Sheep

Baa, baa black sheep,
Have you any wool?
Yes, sir, yes, sir,
Three bags full.
One for my master.
One for my dame.
One for the little boy
Who lives down the lane.

8

9

Chime In

1. Teach the song, using props of three large bags stuffed with paper or fabric scraps.
2. Change the verse to two bags full, to one bag full, and finally to no bags full.
3. Introduce the wall chart.
4. Sing with the wall chart, making changes with word cards.

Read

Pelle's New Suit, Elsa Beskow (Harper and Row).

Drama

1. Have the children make mitten puppets by putting gummed paper circles on their mittens.

Write

1. Have the children make a title page for their individualized *Chime In* Ready for Winter theme books.
2. Make a Story of Wool book. Some children may write about how wool is made. Others might cut out pictures of things made of wool.

Physical Education

1. Take the children on an outdoor walk and watch for animals and birds.
2. As you walk, discuss how animals keep warm, what happens to the flowers, why the trees are bare, and so on.

Wonder Table

Display different kinds of materials, such as wool, silk, leather, fur, vinyl, cotton.
1. Have the children make comparisons: Which is warmest? Which is softest? Which absorbs water?
2. Suggest that the children talk through the material. What happens to sound?

Visit

1. If possible, visit a pioneer museum or crafts shop to see wool spinning.

Mitten Match

1. Place all the children's mittens in a pile. Have the children sort them into pairs.

Creative Arts

1. Have the children weave by using wire mesh for the warp and different fabrics, such as wool, cotton, ribbon, or velvet, as the woof. Be sure to cover the ends of the wire with tape to prevent scratching.
2. The children might paint a picture and then paste on scraps of fabric in some places.

Mathematics

1. Tell subtraction stories.
   (A) Pair students who work with objects such as small blocks.
   (B) A sample dialogue is:

   Student A: We have three blocks.

   Student B: I'll take two.

   Student A: We have one block left.

   (C) Record the stories. The sample dialogue would be recorded as:

Ten Little Squirrels

Ten little,
Nine little,
Eight little squirrels,
Seven little,
Six little,
Five little squirrels,
Four little,
Three little,
Two little squirrels,
One little frisky squirrel.

10

11

Traditional

F

Ten   lit - tle, Nine   lit - tle, Eight   lit - tle squir - rels,

C7   F

Seven lit - tle, Six   lit -tle, Five   lit - tle squir - rels,   Four   lit - tle, Three lit - tle,

C7   F

Two   lit - tle squir - rels,   One   lit - tle Fris - ky   Squir - rel.

Chime In

1. Discuss how animals prepare for Winter.
2. Sing the song with finger play.
3. Sing the first line loudly and each succeeding line a little more softly.
4. Change *squirrels* to other animals. (This may also require changing *frisky* and *little*.)
5. Introduce the wall chart. Use word cards and sing all the variations.
6. Distribute copies of the song.

Watch

1. Show films about animals preparing for Winter.

Read

The Seed the Squirrel Dropped, Haris Petie (Prentice-Hall).

Write

1. Encourage the children to add verses in their individualized *Chime In* theme books.
2. They may also make word cards for numerals and illustrate the cards with gummed circles.

Physical Education

1. Arrange several pieces of equipment (large and small) in the gym. The children may pretend to be busy squirrels responding to directions such as on, off, under, over.
2. Scatter hoops on the floor to represent hollow trees.
3. Develop the concepts of near and far: Run to a tree near you.
4. Listen and move to "Pizzicato" from the *Sylvia Ballet* by Leo Delibes.

Research

1. Allow the children to go to the library to discover how other animals, such as reptiles and birds, spend Winter.
2. They could share this information with the group and the teacher could then record it in a co-operative book.

Creative Arts

1. Use waxed milk cartons or plastic jugs to make bird feeders.

Mathematics

1. Allow the children to work with ten pegs and a pegboard.
   (A) Assign students to work in pairs. One then divides the pegs into two groups on the pegboard and "tells the story" to the other. An example is $4 + 6 = 10$.
   (B) The other copies the "story" (the peg pattern) on another pegboard and then changes the pattern to tell a different story.

Game

1. Play the Squirrels in the Trees game.
   (A) Place all the children except two in scattered groups of three.
   (B) Two of each group join hands to form the tree. The third is the squirrel.
   (C) The two children not assigned to a group are squirrels without trees.
   (D) Play some appropriate music or tap a running rhythm on a tambourine. When the music stops, the squirrels must find a tree. Only one squirrel is allowed per tree. The object of the game is for the children to find a tree before all the trees are occupied.

Big Brown Bear

Big brown bear
You must sleep, sleep, sleep.
Big brown bear
The snow is deep, deep, deep.
Big brown bear
You must sleep, sleep, sleep.

Fly little birds
You must fly, fly, fly.
Fly little birds
Dark and grey the sky.
Fly little birds
You must fly, fly, fly.

12

13

Chime In

1. Teach the song with actions.
2. Make up new verses for other animals.
3. Introduce the wall chart.
4. Mime a verse. Have children guess which animal is represented and then sing the verse with you.

Read

The Biggest Bear, Lynd Ward (Houghton-Mifflin).

Listen

1. Play the *Lullaby* by Johannes Brahms. The children should relax while listening.

Drama

1. Make a cave with blankets.

Write

1. Children may make word cards. Using these and other words in their collections, have them make sentences about animals. Have them read and copy the sentences.

Dramatic Story Telling

Play the Bear Hunt game. It may be staged in the classroom or the gym. Have the children tell a story by repeating your phrases and dramatizing as they do so.

This activity teaches vocabulary, sentence structure, and voice inflection. With experience, the children will soon be the storytellers. This technique may also be used with any story.

Begin by setting a walking pattern. Tell the children to repeat each line after you (or the assigned leader).

Teacher: Let's go on a bear hunt.
Children: Let's go on a bear hunt.

T: I see a wheat field.

C: I see a wheat field.

T: Can't go over. *(Motion with arms while keeping the beat with your feet.)*

C: Can't go over.

T: Can't go under.

C: Can't go under.

T: Let's go through. *(Stop walking. Brush palms together.)*

C: Let's go through.

T: _____ *(Resume walking beat without dialogue.)*

_____

I see a bridge. *(Resume walking.)*

Can't go under.

Can't go around.

Let's go over. *(Thump chest.)*
_____ *(Resume walking.)*

_____

I see some mud.

Can't go over.

Can't go under.

Let's go through. *(Walk slowly, making mud sounds with mouth.)*

_____ *(Resume walking.)*

_____

Scared?

Not much.

I see a lake.

Can't go over.

Can't go under.

Let's go through.   (*Make swimming
                            motions, then
                            resume walking.*)

_____

_____

I see a tree.

Can't go over.

Can't go under.

Let's go up.   (*Make climbing
                            motion.*)

I don't see any bears.   (*Shade eyes. Look
                            around. Climb
                            down.*)

_____   (*Resume walking.*)

_____

I see a cave.

Can't go over.

Can't go under.

Let's go in.   (*Whisper. Walk on
                            tip-toe.*)

_____

_____

I see two eyes.

I see a nose.

IT'S A BEAR.   (*Run back home.*)

Theme Unit 5
Winter Festivities

Winter Festivities Resource Record

Resources Available	Comments
Books and Other Print Materials	
Films, Filmstrips, and Other Non-print Materials	

Resources Available	Comments
Records and Tapes	
People in the Community	
Other (Including Equipment)	

14

Teddy Bear

Teddy bear, teddy bear,
Turn around.
Teddy bear, teddy bear,
Touch the ground.
Teddy bear, teddy bear,
Show your shoe.
Teddy bear, teddy bear,
That will do.

Teddy bear, teddy bear,
Climb upstairs.
Teddy bear, teddy bear,
Say your prayers.
Teddy bear, teddy bear,
Turn off the light.
Teddy bear, teddy bear,
Say good-night.

15

Chime In

1. Teach the poem with actions.
2. Have the children bring their teddy bears or use stick puppet bears to dramatize the song.
3. Make substitutes for teddy bear (such as names of well-known doll figures).
4. Ask what else the teddy bear could do. Sample answers are shake my hand, dance a jig, nod its head.
5. Distribute copies of the poem.

Read

Winnie the Pooh and the Honey Tree, A. A. Milne (Western).

Dramatic Story Telling

1. Tell the story of *The Three Bears* using the Bear Hunt game technique (see p. 75).

Write

1. Have the children make a title page for their individualized *Chime In* Winter Festivities theme books.
2. Have the children write a letter to a teddy bear inviting it to a party. Decide on a day and time, and print this on a chart for the children to copy.

Plan the Party

Have the children help you plan the party entertainment.

1. What game would the teddy bears like to play?
2. What story would they like to hear?
3. What song could the children sing for their teddy bears?
4. What record would the teddy bears like to hear?

Physical Education

1. The children may chant the poem as they skip or bounce a ball.
2. Listen and move to *The Nutcracker Suite*, Peter Tchaikovsky. Encourage the children to use all the space and move at different levels when the toys come to life. At the sound of a bell, they must rush back to the "shelf" because the shop-keeper has returned.

Wonder Table

1. Display favourite toys. Prepare labels (Jenny's boat, Bobby's train, etc.)
2. Classify the toys (toys that move, toys made of plastic, quiet toys, noisy toys).

Creative Arts

1. Make party hats.
2. Make stick puppets. Cut out teddy bear shapes and glue a wooden stick (popsicle stick or tongue depressor) on the back. Use coloured paper or paint the teddy shapes.
3. Set up a toy shop window. Paint and cut out toy shapes and make toys with boxes. Pin the toys on a mural.

Mathematics

1. Price the toys by visiting a store or checking catalogues.
2. Make price tags for toys in the shop window mural.

The Toy Store

Let's go to the store today.
We will find our favourite toys.
There's a rocking-horse for us to ride.
We would like to stay and play.
We would like to stay and play.
We would like to stay and play.

5

Chime In

1. Teach the song by rote.
2. Add sound effects. Half the class should make clicking noises with their tongues while the others sing. They may also use lummi sticks to tap as they sing.
3. Have the children suggest other things in the room that would make good sound effects.
4. Add other verses.
5. Introduce the wall chart.

Discuss

1. Talk about other ways children can cause toys to move.

Read

Mr. Willowby's Christmas, Robert Barry (McGraw-Hill).

Write

1. Add new verses by colouring, copying, or writing.
2. Have the children write advertisements for the toys in the toy store mural.

Tape Commercials

1. The teacher should work with small groups to collect ideas and edit them orally. Have each group tape its commercial.

Physical Education

1. Set up the Jingle Bell dance in the classroom or gym. Have the children form one large circle.

Dashing through the snow   (*Circle to the right.*)

In a one-horse open sleigh,

O'er the field we go,   (*Circle to the left.*)

Laughing all the way;

Bells on bobtail ring,	(*Half move into centre.*)
Making spirits bright,	(*Then move back.*)
What fun it is to ride and sing	(*Other half move into centre.*)
A sleighing song tonight!	(*Then move back.*)
Jingle bells,	(*Clap hands in front.*)
Jingle bells,	(*Clap hands behind.*)
Jingle all the way!	(*Clap hands on thighs.*)
Oh, what fun it is to ride	(*Circle to the right.*)

In a one-horse open sleigh!

2. Print the words to Jingle Bells on a wall chart. Read them and sing the song with the children.

Wonder Table

1. Display a globe and stamps from several countries.
   (A) Talk about the Christmas stamp edition.
   (B) Have the children watch for interesting stamps to add to the display.

This activity may continue for a few weeks to lead into Valentines and Mail (Theme Unit 8).

Creative Arts

Make "gingerbread houses" from used seasonal greeting cards.

1. The teacher or a parent volunteer should prepare the house pieces in advance. Cut cards into rectangles and staple three thicknesses together for strength. Show a design on both sides (top and bottom).

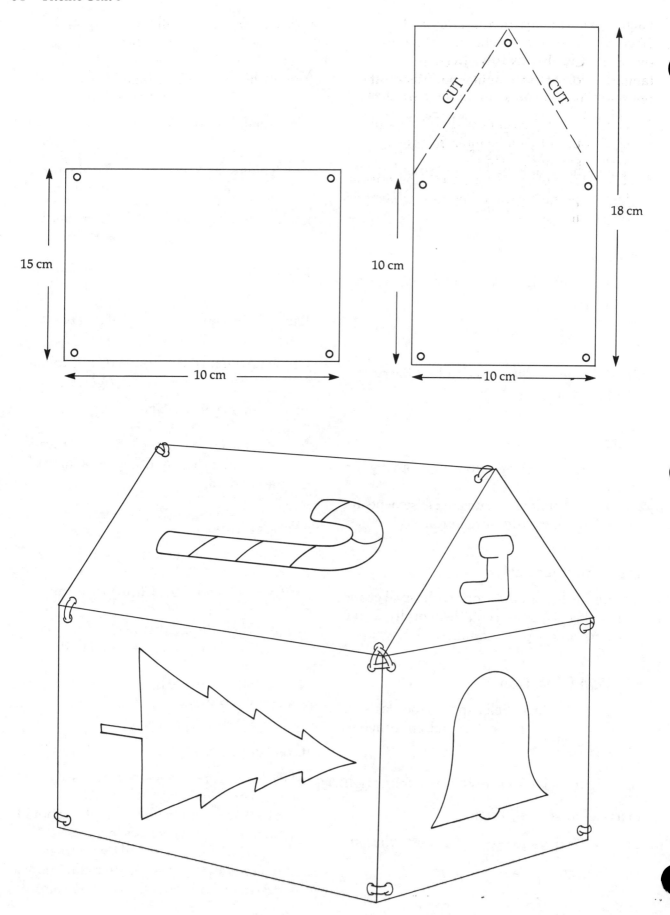

Each house will require 5 rectangles of 10 cm by 15 cm and 2 rectangles of 10 cm by 18 cm. Cut the 10 cm by 18 cm rectangles to form the triangular roof shape at one end. Punch holes at joining points.

2. Have the children choose their house pieces by colour or theme (winter, religious symbols, humour, etc.).

3. They start with the base and tie the sides at joining points by threading through lengths of coloured wool.

4. The children may fill their completed houses with cookies or candies and take them home as a family present. (Many of these houses have become family treasures which are brought out year after year.)

Come to the Parade

Come to the parade
Come to the parade
Come to the parade.
What will we see?

Clowns walking upside down
Clowns walking upside down
Clowns walking upside down.
Funny, funny clowns.

Santa Claus waving
Santa Claus waving
Santa Claus waving.
Ho, ho, ho, ho, ho.

Chime In

1. Teach the song and dramatize the answers.
2. Introduce the wall chart.
3. Have children take turns holding up their answers for the class to sing (if you do the writing activity).
4. Distribute copies of the song.

Read

Bah! Humbug?, Lorna Balion (Abingdon Press).

Listen

Play records of Christmas and other seasonal songs.

Write

1. Place long strips of construction paper in the writing centre.
2. Have the children print an answer to the song.
3. Use the answer strips as a border around the parade mural.

Physical Education

1. Provide xylophones or rhythm sticks. Have the children tap out rhythms to represent something in the parade song. For example, one group could tap rhythm sticks as they say:

Clówns   Clówns   Clówns

Another group may join in, adding a description but keeping the beat:

Fúnny Clówns   Fúnny Clówns   Fúnny Clówns

Visit

1. Take the class to see seasonal store decorations.
2. Take the class to a woodlot to buy a tree.
3. Take them to a supermarket to buy ingredients for cookies.

What Is It?

1. Place a Christmas decoration in a bag. Have one child reach in and describe what he or she feels. The other children must try to guess what it is.

Creative Arts

1. Make a background for the parade mural. Cut shapes of buildings from the classified ad section of a newspaper. Use black markers to indicate windows and doors.
2. Paint pictures of the parade. Cut out figures and paste them on the mural.

Mathematics

1. Follow a recipe to make Christmas cookies. Ask a parent volunteer to supervise small groups.

Carol of the Beasts

Jesus, our Brother, kind and good,
Was humbly born in a stable rude.
And the friendly beasts around him stood.
Jesus, our Brother, kind and good.

"I" said the donkey, shaggy and brown,
"I carried His mother uphill and down;
"I carried His mother to Bethlehem town.
"I" said the donkey, shaggy and brown.

"I" said the cow all white and red,
"I gave Him my manger for His bed;
"I gave Him my hay to pillow his head.
"I" said the cow, all white and red.

10

11

"I" said the sheep with curly horn,
"I gave Him my wool for His blanket warm.
"He wore my coat on Christmas morn.
"I" said the sheep with curly horn.

"I" said the dove from the rafters high,
"Cooed Him to sleep that He should not cry;
"We cooed Him to sleep, my mate and I.
"I" said the dove from the rafters high.

12

13

Chime In

1. Teach the song using pictures to represent the verses.
2. Divide children into groups to represent the animals.
3. Sing with the wall chart.
4. Draw attention to the quotation marks.
5. For variety, have the children sing only the words in quotation marks. You sing the others.
6. Distribute copies of the song.

Read

A variety of seasonal greeting cards.

Write

1. Make Christmas Is. . . . booklets. Each page should be headed Christmas Is. . . .

Film

Show *The Twelve Days of Christmas.*

Physical Education

Play the Pathways game.
1. Have the children draw shapes to show the path the donkey may have travelled (for example, straight, curved, zigzag).
2. Have the children exchange pathway sheets. See if they can follow the path which another child has drawn.

Discuss

1. Talk about sharing time, friendship, and things.
2. Talk about the sights, smells, tastes, and sounds of the season.

Share

1. Have the children bring a small gift for a child in a hospital. (Or you could help them arrange a bake sale to buy some little gifts.)
2. The children may wrap them during activity time.
3. Ask the school nurse or a parent volunteer to deliver them on behalf of the class.

Creative Arts

1. Make a variety of decorations for the tree. Examples are: tissue paper balls (pinch circles in the middle, thread through a stack, then tie the two thread ends together to form a ball); angels (use a clothespin or a plastic spoon and cover with a paper doilie, then use pipe cleaners for arms and silver doilies for wings); chains (string cranberries and popcorn).

Mathematics

1. Give children a pegboard and pegs. Have them place two red pegs on the board and use blue pegs to make a path between the two red pegs. Then have them use yellow pegs to make an alternate path. Which path is longer? Which is shorter?

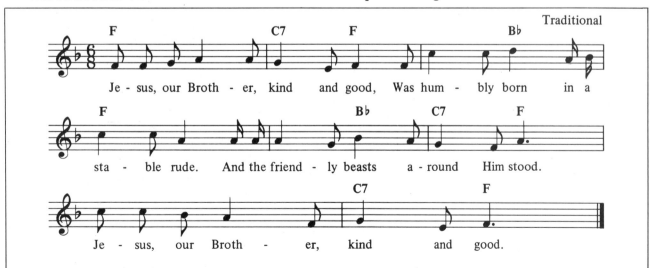

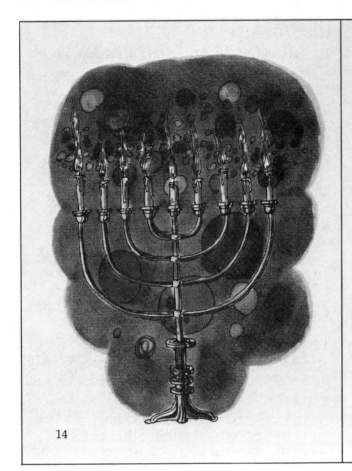

14

Hanukkah Lights

1 light, 2 lights, 3 lights, 4
5 lights, 6 lights, and 3 more.
Twinkle, twinkle,
9 pretty lights
In a golden menorah bright.

15

Chime In

1. Teach the poem as a finger play.
2. Show the children a menorah.
3. Recite the poem as you place candles in the menorah.
4. Introduce the wall chart and read the poem again.
5. Cover the numerals with word cards, and read it again.

Read

Hanukkah Money, Sholem Aleichem (Greenwillow Publishers).

The Story of Hanukkah

1. Place story sequence cards at the listening centre. Children should arrange them in the correct order, and then tape their story.

Discuss

1. Talk about the different ways in which people celebrate the season.
2. Talk about the concept that special days are a time to show that we love one another.

Listen

1. Play records of songs and stories dealing with religious and seasonal celebrations of other ethnic groups.

Wonder Table

1. Display different sizes of bells. The children will enjoy listening to the different sounds.

Creative Arts

1. Make a dreydl with a square cardboard box. Print a Hebrew letter on each side of the box.

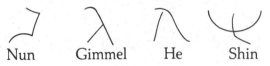

Nun   Gimmel   He   Shin

2. The letters are pronounced as:
   Nun   Gimmel   Hay   Sheen
3. The translation is:
   A great   miracle   happened   there.

Play

Tell the children the origin of the Dreydl game.

When the Jewish people were forbidden to study the Torah, many brave teachers secretly gathered the children together in order to teach them. They sat around a bare table with a dredyl in the centre. If a soldier happened to come in, they would spin the dreydl and pretend to be playing a game.

Set up the Dreydl game. There are two versions. Pieces of fruit may be used in place of popcorn for prizes.

1. Have the children make a number of small bundles of popcorn for prizes. Give each child two or three bundles and put a few more in a pile. Each child takes a turn at spinning the dreydl.
   (A) If *Nun* is facing up when it stops spinning, the child gets no prize.
   (B) If *Heh* is facing up, the child receives half the pile as a prize.
   (C) If *Shin* is facing up, the child puts one of his or her own bundle in the pile.
   (D) If *Gimmel* is facing up, the child receives the whole pile as a prize.
2. Rather than using bundles of popcorn as prizes, the children keep a running score.
   (A) If *Nun* is facing up, the score is zero.
   (B) If *Heh* is facing up, the score is 5.
   (C) If *Shin* is facing up, the score is *minus* 1.
   (D) If *Gimmel* is facing up, the score is 10.

Ay   Ay

ay   ay   ay   ay
Look out of my way.
ee   ee   ee   ee
Make room for little me.
ie   ie   ie   ie

I can't see, now it's no lie!
oe   oe   oe   oe
Did I stand on your big toe?
ue   ue   ue   ue
I am sorry, that is true.
ay   ee   ie   oe   ue   Boo!

Chime In

1. Tell the children that this song was composed with a group of children who had just been to a parade.
2. Sing the song.
3. Introduce the wall chart.
4. Preface the vowel sound with any appropriate consonant or blend.
5. Leave the song chart and small cards for substitution at the language centre.
6. The children will enjoy looking for these vowel sounds in their books.

Theme Unit 6
Telling Time

Telling Time Resource Record

Resources Available	*Comments*
Books and Other Print Materials	
Films, Filmstrips, and Other Non-print Materials	

Resources Available	Comments
Records and Tapes	
People in the Community	
Other (Including Equipment)	

Hickory Dickory Dock

Hickory dickory dock,
The mouse ran up the clock.
The clock struck one.
The mouse ran down.
Hickory, dickory, dock.

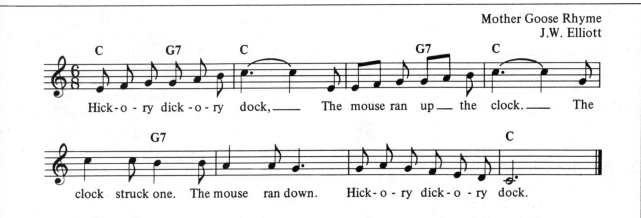

Mother Goose Rhyme
J.W. Elliott

Hick-o-ry dick-o-ry dock,___ The mouse ran up__ the clock.___ The

clock struck one. The mouse ran down. Hick-o-ry dick-o-ry dock.

Chime In

1. Sing with actions.
2. Have some children make clock sounds as others sing. Use wood blocks, sticks, triangles, etc.
3. Sing with the wall chart.
4. Replace *one* with other numeral words.
5. Distribute copies of the song.

Discuss

1. Talk about other ways of telling time (by the sun, by shadows).
2. Take the class outside early and late in the day. Compare the positions of the sun and shadows.

Read

What Makes a Shadow?, Clyde Bulla (Thomas Y. Crowell).

Write

1. Have the children make a title page for their individualized *Chime In* Telling Time theme books.
2. Some children may make word cards.
3. Some children may write or tell a story about the mouse. Why did it run? Where did it go?

Physical Education

1. Lead the children through the song with actions.

Hickory, dickory, dock.	(*Swing arms like a pendulum.*)
The mouse ran up the clock.	(*Reach up.*)
The clock struck one.	(*Clap hands.*)
The mouse ran down.	(*Bring arms down.*)
Hickory, dickory, dock.	(*Swing arms like a pendulum.*)

2. Have the children listen and move to *The Syncopated Clock*, Anderson, and *Shadow Dance, 2nd Modern Suite, Opus 14*, Edward MacDowell.
3. Play Shadow Walk in the classroom or gym. Children work in pairs. One copies the other's actions.
4. Play Shadow Tag out of doors. One is designated "it". "It" tries to step on another's shadow. When successful, the child whose shadow was stepped on becomes "it".

5. Play the What Time is It, Oh, Wolf? game. The teacher or a child leads a group which repeatedly asks, "What time is it, oh, wolf?" The "wolf" leader answers, "3 o'clock", "10 o'clock", etc. But when the wolf answers, "Dinner time!", the group runs for home. The wolf gives chase and tags someone who then becomes the wolf.

Family Schedules

1. Have parents help the child record the family's schedule. The child may then share and compare schedules with other children.

Creative Arts

1. The children may make mouse puppets with an old sock. Collect pieces of felt, wool, and other fabric scraps to make mouse features.

Mathematics

1. Make Clock books for each child. Cut off the top half of the inside pages. On the upper half of the inside back cover, mount a moveable clock hand and draw a clock face with numerals. (Use the 12 h clock face at this early stage.) Have the children print one sentence on each half page. An example is "I go to bed at 8 o'clock." As the child turns the pages, he or she moves the hands of the clock to fit the sentence.

2. Strike a triangle to represent a clock chiming. The children then move their clock hands to show what time it is. (This may be used with hours and half hours.)

Star Light

Star light,
Star bright,
First star I've seen tonight.
I wish I may,
I wish I might,
Have the wish I wish tonight.

5

Chime In

1. Chant the poem with a clapping pattern.
2. Have the children change the pattern (by clapping hands to knees, hands to head, etc.).
3. Introduce the wall chart. Encourage the children to find all the words that look and sound like *light*.
4. Chant the poem, giving three children a chance to make a wish. Repeat.
5. Talk about other ways of making wishes (wishing wells, wishbones, blowing out birthday candles, pulling crackers).
6. Distribute copies of the poem.

Read

The Magic Fish, Freya Littledale (Scholastic).
Chicken Soup With Rice, Maurice Sendak (Scholastic).
No School Today, Franz Brandenberg (Macmillan).

Write

1. The children may add I Wish pages to their theme books. One way is to draw shapes of mice, cats, etc., with balloons for dialogue. The balloons may then be filled with such wishes as: I wish (I had some cheese), I wish (I had a mouse), etc.

Physical Education

1. Have the children listen and relax to *Clair De Lune*, Claude Debussy.
2. Have them play skipping or ball bouncing games. They chant:

   Apples, peaches, pears, plums,

   Tell me when your birthday comes.

   January, February . . . ."

Each child joins in when his or her birthday month is called. Don't expect all the children to know the months; however, hearing them now will make them more familiar and easier to learn.

Wonder Table

1. Display an old and a new calendar, different kinds of calendars and diaries, etc.
2. Make a wall chart for Happy New Year To You (sung to the tune of *Happy Birthday to You*). Display the chart near the wonder table.

Nature Walk

1. Have the children write star-shaped invitations to their parents for a night walk and then a visit to the school for refreshments.
2. Help the children prepare cookies shaped as suns, moons, and stars for the party.

Creative Arts

1. Make a crayon resist.
   (A) Colour a page.
   (B) Paint over the page with black tempera paint.
   (C) Etch a design by scraping some of the paint off.
2. Make crackers using toilet paper rolls. Each child prints a "wish come true" and puts it in the roll. Wrap the rolls with crepe paper and decorate.

Mathematics

1. Give the children a January calendar. They may fill in the names of the days and the numerals.
2. Have them compare their calendars with other months at the wonder table.

Theme Unit 7
Winter

Winter Resource Record

Resources Available	Comments
Books and Other Print Materials	
Films, Filmstrips, and Other Non-print Materials	

Resources Available	Comments
Records and Tapes	
People in the Community	
Other (Including Equipment)	

Snowflakes

Snowflakes are filling,
Are filling the air.
Look at the footprints
I see over there.
Was it a rabbit
Or was it a bear?
Come let us follow it
Back to its lair.

6

7

J.M.

Tune: Pussy Cat, Pussy Cat

Snow-flakes are fill - ing, Are fill - ing the air.   Look at the foot-prints I

see o - ver there.   Was it a rab - bit Or was it a bear?

Come let us fol - low it Back to its lair.

Chime In

1. Show the children pictures of animal tracks, and have them guess to which animal they belong.
2. Teach the song.
3. Introduce the wall chart.
4. Which animals would leave tracks in the snow? Change the names in the song and sing it again.
5. Birds leave tracks, too. Change the names to names of birds and sing again.
6. Distribute copies of the song.

Read

"Follow, Follow" from *It's Winter*, Sister Noemi Weygant (Westminster Press).

Write

1. Have the children make a title page for their individualized *Chime In* Winter theme books.
2. Write or tell a story of following animal tracks. Where did they lead? What did you see on the way?

Bird Feeders

1. If you used the Creative Arts activity for *Ten Little Squirrels* (see p. 73), ask the children what kinds of food they are putting in their bird feeders.

Physical Education

1. Have the children listen and move to "The Snow is Dancing" from *Children's Corner Suite*, Claude Debussy.
2. Take the children for an outdoor walk:
   (A) Look for footprints.
   (B) Follow each other's footprints.
   (C) Take the temperature of surface snow and of deep snow.
   (D) Catch snowflakes on black paper. Look at them through a magnifying glass.

Wonder Table

1. The children may fill several jars with snow and leave them on the table. How many jars of snow make one jar of water?
2. Compare the mass of a jar of fluffy snow to a jar of firmly packed snow. (You may wish to use the term *weight* rather than *mass* with this age group.)

Creative Arts

1. Make a Winter mural with cutouts of snowflakes, snow figures, children skating, skiing, tobogganning, etc.
2. Cut wide strips of dark paper for the border. Have the children step on or put their hands in white paint and make their prints on the border. Ask a parent volunteer to stand by with a basin of water.

Mathematics

1. Make a large thermometer. Have children show how cold the snow was, what the temperature is, etc.
2. Make individual books to record snow experiment results. An option is to record results in their individualized *Chime In* books.

The Snowman

I made a great tall snowman
With two huge coal black eyes
And just to reach around his neck
Took two of daddy's ties.
I put a hat of mother's
Upon his rounded head
And then I ran and left him
And hurried off to bed.
When I awoke next morning
Imagine my surprise
My snowman had run away
And left his hat, ties, and eyes!

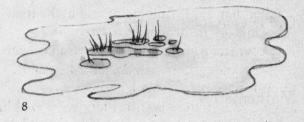

8

9

Chime In

1. Use a flannel board. Make a felt snow figure and other things to add.
2. Teach the poem.
3. Have the children take turns making the snowman as the poem is recited.
4. Introduce the wall chart. Read the poem and discuss the "'s" in the words *daddy's* and *mother's*.
5. Distribute copies of the poem. Read it with the children.

Read

The Summer Snowman, Gene Zion (Harper and Row).
Katy and the Big Snow, Virginia Lee Burton (Houghton-Mifflin).

Write

1. Laminate pictures of children playing in the snow. Have the children choose a picture and write or tell a story about it. If a child is not able to write independently, the teacher should print the story for the child and leave a space below in which he or she may copy it.
2. Give each child a copy of We Are Going Out to Play (see the Physical Education activity). They may add more verses.

Display Chart

1. Have each child bring a very small article to tape on a chart.
2. Prepare labels for each (Debbie's picture, Bobby's pencil, etc.).

Physical Education

1. Sing We Are Going Out to Play to the tune of *London Bridge*, and have a child mime an "answer". The other children should guess what the answer is and copy it as they all sing the song.

We are going out to play,

Out to play, out to play.

We are going out to play.

What shall we do today?

We will go skating,

Skating, skating,

We will go skating,

That's what we'll do today.

2. Take the children outdoors to make a snow figure family, a snow scene on a brick wall, etc.

Creative Arts

1. Blow white paint with a straw to make trees and bushes on a dark background.
2. Whip soap flakes with enough water so that the mixture is stiff. Place some on blue or foil paper. Brush or use fingers to make a snow scene.

Mathematics

1. Have the children make snow figure addition stories — felt snow figures decorated with buttons are ideal. The children should record their stories in their mathematics books.

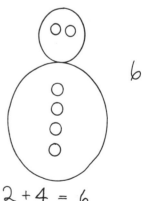

$$2 + 4 = 6$$

2. Have the children make a design with round attribute blocks and then trace and colour it.
3. How many round things can the children find in the classroom?

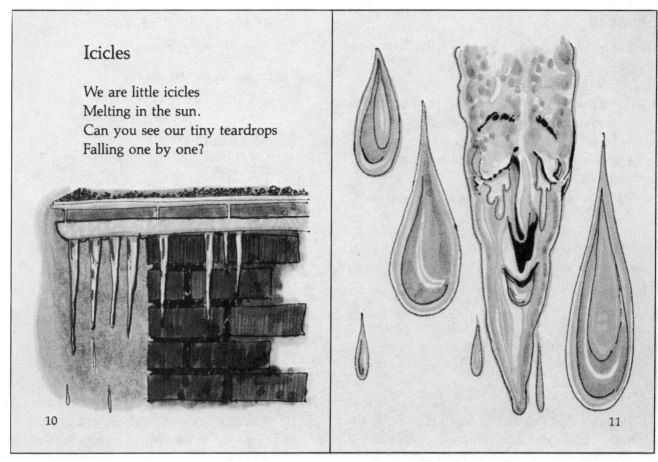

Icicles

We are little icicles
Melting in the sun.
Can you see our tiny teardrops
Falling one by one?

10

11

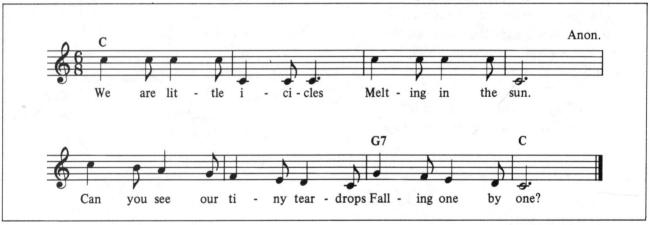

Anon.

C

We   are   lit - tle   i - ci - cles   Melt - ing   in   the   sun.

G7   C

Can   you   see   our   ti - ny tear - drops Fall - ing one   by   one?

Chime In

1. Bring an icicle into the classroom. Hold it over aluminum foil, paper, or water.
2. Choose a child to demonstrate on an instrument the sound of the icicle dripping.
3. Have the group chant "drip, drip" as you recite the poem.
4. Ask the children to think of other words to describe melting. They may take turns accompanying their chanting, using musical instruments, body parts, or objects in the room.
5. Emphasize "-ing" words.
6. Distribute copies of the song.

Read

In The Flaky Frosty Morning, Karla Kuskin (Harper and Row).

Write

1. Have the children look for "-ing" words in their Chime In books or other books.
2. They may copy these "-ing" words on long rolls of paper, such as an adding machine tape or toilet paper. Making the tape as long as possible will add to the fun.

Physical Education

1. How many ways can the children find of moving down? Provide a variety of equipment for them to demonstrate their answers.

Theme Unit 8
Valentines and Mail

Valentines and Mail Resource Record

Resources Available	Comments
Books and Other Print Materials	
Films, Filmstrips, and Other Non-print Materials	

Resources Available	Comments
Records and Tapes	
People in the Community	
Other (Including Equipment)	

Love Somebody

Love somebody, yes, I do.
Love somebody, yes, I do.
Love somebody, yes, I do.
Love somebody, but I won't tell who!

Chime In

1. Teach the song as a game. Children sit in circle with hands behind their backs. One child closes his or her eyes. Another walks around as the song is sung and places a Valentine in someone's hand. The child then opens his or her eyes and has three guesses to find who has the Valentine.
2. Distribute copies of the song.

Read

A Letter to Amy, Ezra J. Keats (Harper and Row).
St. Valentine's Day, Clyde Robert Bulla (Thomas Y. Crowell).

Write

1. Have the children make a title page for their individualized *Chime In* Valentines and Mail theme books.
2. Provide a selection of old Valentine cards.
3. Children may make cards for their classmates. Some may copy verses; others may write their own.
4. "Mail" them in the classroom mailbox. Each day, choose a child to deliver them to the correct envelopes (see the Creative Arts activity).

Mail

1. Have the children make Valentines for their parents.
2. Provide envelopes and an address list so that the children may copy the address for mailing.

Visit

1. Take the children to the post office to buy stamps. Have them stamp and mail their Valentines.
2. If this is impractical, bring stamps to the classroom, but still have the children stamp and mail their Valentines.

Physical Education

1. Play the Mail at My Door game.
   (A) Have the children bring a name card to the gym. Spread these around the perimeter of the room.
   (B) Choose a child to be the letter carrier of four letters.
   (C) As the children walk and sing, "As I was walking down the street," the letter carrier delivers the mail to the proper "houses".
   (D) As the children sing, "I saw some mail at my door," those who see mail "at their door" go and sit down.
   (E) Continue until everyone has mail.
2. These are the lyrics. Sing to the tune of *Rig-a-Jig-Jig*:

As I was walking down the street,

Down the street, down the street,

As I was walking down the street,

Hi ho, hi ho, hi ho.

I saw some mail at my door,

At my door, at my door,

I saw some mail at my door,

Hi ho, hi ho, hi ho.

Creative Arts

1. Have the children make large Valentine envelopes. Sew the sides and print their names in large letters. Decorate the envelopes.
2. Clothespeg all the envelopes to a rope. Leave on display until Valentine's Day.

Mathematics

1. Have the children make houses for a mural. Number the houses clearly. Use odd numbers on one side of the street and even numbers on the other.
2. Count by 2's, odds and evens.
3. Add letter carriers, delivery trucks, etc., to the mural.

14

Letters

Some letters go by plane,
Plane, plane.
Some letters go by train,
Train, train.
But my letter's taking a trip,
Trip, trip
On a great big ship.

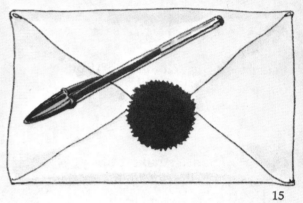

15

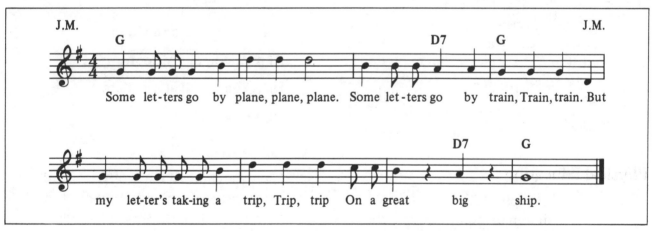

Chime In

1. Introduce the song by showing pictures of mail being loaded on planes, trains, and ships.
2. Teach the song and have the children point to the appropriate pictures as they sing.
3. Sing with the wall chart.
4. Add sound effects as accompaniment to the singing.
5. Emphasize the "tr" blend in train and trip.
6. Make substitutes in the *Lappy Lappy* song (see p. 60).

Read

Freight Train, D. Crews (Greenwillow Publishers).

Write

1. The children may make a book about transportation. Use one page of the book for each mode. Arrange the pages from the slowest to the fastest form of transportation.

Visit

1. If possible, take the children to an airport to see mail being loaded and luggage being weighed.

Physical Education

Introduce the concepts of faster and slower.
1. Have the children demonstrate how they can make a hoop, rope, or ball move slowly or quickly.
2. Set a beat with a drum or tambourine. Have the children walk to the beat. Vary by gradually slowing down or quickening the beat.

Wonder Table

1. Display the stamps that the children have collected. Sort them by face value, colour, or country.

Creative Arts

1. Collect scraps of wood from a lumber yard or vocational class. The children may use them to make planes, trains, etc., and then paint their products.
2. Have children tell or write how they made their objects.

Mathematics

1. Make a post office. The children may make signs telling about the cost of the stamps, opening and closing times, etc.
2. The children may also wrap and weigh parcels, make stamps and air mail stickers, and so on.
3. Have the children make train tickets, marking the destination and price of the trip.

Train Ride

If possible, arrange for the class to take a short train ride.
1. Have the children fill out a baggage ticket in advance and pin it on before leaving.
2. Discuss the cost of tickets (the farther you go, the more it costs).
3. Give each child a schedule so that he or she can see prices.

Theme Unit 9
Health

Health Resource Record

Resources Available	Comments
Books and Other Print Materials	
Films, Filmstrips, and Other Non-print Materials	

Resources Available	Comments
Records and Tapes	
People in the Community	
Other (Including Equipment)	

Johnny, Get Your Hair Cut

Johnny, get your hair cut
Hair cut, hair cut
Johnny, get your hair cut
Just like me.

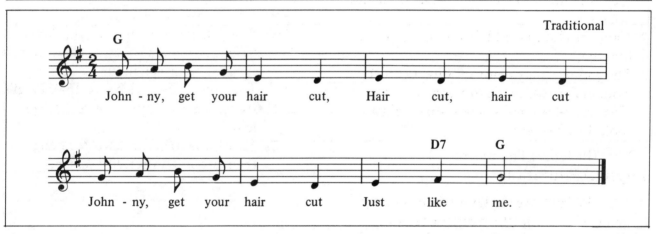

Chime In

1. Teach the song. Play an accompaniment on a xylophone using E and D. Have some children chant "hair cut, hair cut" while the others sing the song.
2. What else could Johnny do to make himself look nice?
3. One group could sing a question, and a second group could reply. Sample dialogue is: Did you brush your teeth? Yes, I brushed my teeth.
4. Distribute copies of the song.

Read

Harry The Dirty Dog, Gene Zion (Harper and Row).
Weighing and Balancing, Jane Jonas Srivastava (Fitzhenry & Whiteside).

Write

1. Have the children make a title page for their individualized *Chime In* Health theme books.
2. Have the children add their own verses to the song.
3. The children may enjoy cutting pictures from magazines to illustrate their verses. (Examples are combs, soap, shoe polish, tooth brushes, etc.)

Physical Education

1. Play the Here We Go Looby Loo singing game. (For complete instructions, see *Singing Games for Children*, Hamlin and Guessford, Willis Music Co.)
2. Play the This Is The Way We Brush Our Teeth game (sung to the tune of *Here We Go Round the Mulberry Bush*). Use variations, such as cutting nails, washing faces, etc.
3. Have the children listen and move to *Polonaise*, J. S. Bach. Have the children think about their posture as they move.

Puppet Show

1. Discuss good manners.
2. Have the children demonstrate good manners with puppets.

Wonder Table

1. Place some scales near the table. Have the children weigh themselves and record their mass on a chart.

Creative Arts

1. Give the children large sheets of mural paper. While one lies down on the paper, another traces the child's figure. The children may add features and clothing by painting.
2. These figures may be cut out and taped to the children's chairs for open house.

Mathematics

1. The children may make a bar graph to show their various heights.
   (A) When they make the Creative Arts tracing figures, have them cut a strip showing their heights as well.
   (B) The children may decorate their height strips and print their names in large letters.
   (C) Tape these strips on a wall or hang them around an activity centre.

My Wobbly Tooth

I bit my apple
And what do you think?
My wobbly tooth
Came out in a wink.
If I put it under my pillow tonight,
Will the tooth fairy come
When I turn out the light?

5

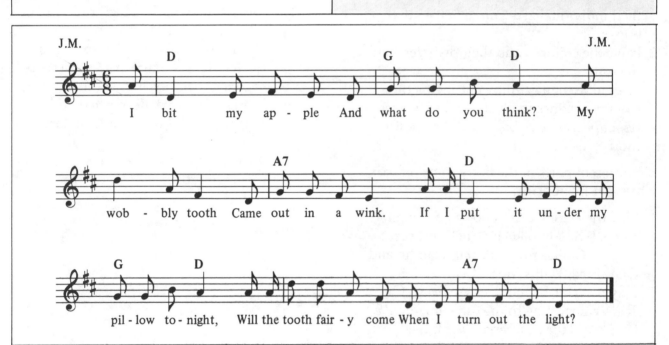

Chime In

1. Discuss losing baby teeth and why it is important to look after our teeth.
2. Before singing the song, put a coin under a pillow. Then sing the song. Have a child look under the pillow and tell what coin is found.
3. The children close their eyes as another coin is hidden. Sing the song and choose another child to find the coin.
4. Introduce the wall chart. Emphasize "-ink" words.
5. Distribute copies of the song.

Read

Heather's Feathers, Leattie Weiss (Franklin Watts).

Write

1. Display pictures of dentists and dental hygiene.
2. Children may write stories about a visit to the dentist or about losing their baby teeth.

Physical Education

1. For listening and relaxing, play *Sea Gulls*, Hap Palmer. Direct the children to tighten their fists, then relax. Continue naming different parts of the body to be tensed and then relaxed.
2. Give each child a feather. Who can keep it in the air the longest by blowing?

Wonder Table

1. Display such objects as a baby tooth, an animal's tooth, and a set of false teeth.

Guest Visit

1. Invite a dental hygenist or dentist to talk about care of teeth.

Visit

1. If possible, visit a dentist's office.

Creative Arts

1. Have children cut out pictures of a variety of foods.
   (A) Place some feathers and the cutouts on a large piece of paper.
   (B) Use a tooth brush and wire mesh to spatter paint over the arrangement. (Place the wire mesh a few centimetres above the paper.)

Mathematics

1. Have the children make a number of paper feathers.

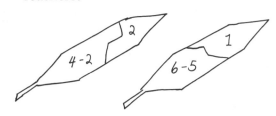

2. Children may write their subtraction stories on the feathers. When they have been checked for accuracy, the feathers may be cut into story puzzles.

One Red Spot

My fever was high.
I felt so hot.
And on my nose
Was one red spot.

My spot grew bigger.
My face turned blue.
I asked the doctor,
"What shall I do?"

The doctor said,
"Here's a purple pill.
Take it in the morning
So you won't get ill."

6

7

I took that pill
And I washed it down
With a choke and a squirm
And I made a frown.

The spot went away
To my great delight
So I told everybody,
"I'm all right!"

8

9

Chime In

1. Have the children tell about when they were sick.
2. Discuss how fortunate we are to have doctors to help us.
3. Discuss ways to keep healthy.
4. Recite the poem for the children.
5. Have the children lie down and pretend to be sick. As you read the last verse, they may jump up and join in on the last line.
6. When the children are able to recite the poem, choose half the group to take the role of the child and the other half to take the role of the doctor.

Read

Curious George Goes to the Hospital, Margaret Rey (Houghton-Mifflin).

Write

1. Have the children write Get Well cards for any class member who is sick.
2. Have the children write prescriptions,
3. Make shopping lists of good foods for good health.

Creative Arts

1. Have the children make a design with paint using eye droppers, empty hypodermic needles, and cotton swabs.
2. The children could make a collage of good foods for good health.

Listen

Play "Spoonful of Sugar" from *Mary Poppins.*

Drama

1. Provide doctor and nurse kits, crutches, bandages, etc., in the play area.
2. If there is a wheelchair available in the school, have the children take turns sitting in it so that they can gain some appreciation for a handicapped child's sensitivities when surrounded by active, healthy children. This will also help them overcome the strangeness and fear that they might feel if they should ever find themselves in a hospital environment.

Mathematics

1. Provide measuring spoons at the sand table. The children will discover that a "spoonful" could mean a small amount or a large amount, and so one must be told what size of spoon to use.

Theme Unit 10
Weather

Weather Resource Record

Resources Available	Comments
Books and Other Print Materials	
Films, Filmstrips, and Other Non-print Materials	

Resources Available	Comments
Records and Tapes	
People in the Community	
Other (Including Equipment)	

Five Kites

1,   2,   3,   4,   5
Five little kites flying up in the sky
Said "Hi" to the clouds as they passed by;
Said "Hi" to the birds,
Said "Hi" to the sun,
Said "Hi" to an airplane,
"Oh, what fun."
Then swish went the wind,
And they all took a dive
5,   4,   3,   2,   1.

10

11

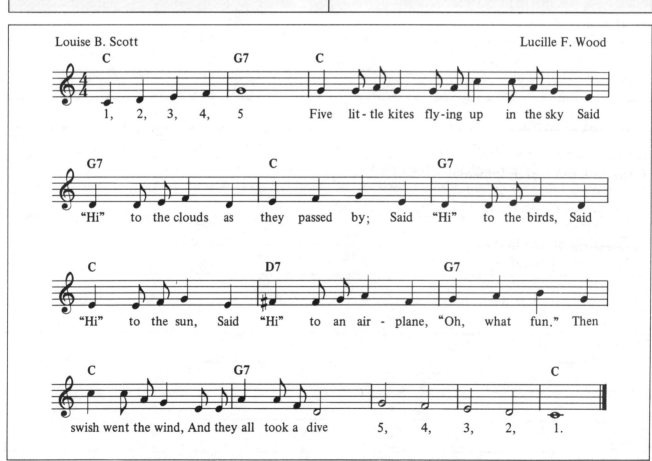

Louise B. Scott   Lucille F. Wood

1, 2, 3, 4, 5 Five lit-tle kites fly-ing up in the sky Said

"Hi" to the clouds as they passed by; Said "Hi" to the birds, Said

"Hi" to the sun, Said "Hi" to an air-plane, "Oh, what fun." Then

swish went the wind, And they all took a dive 5, 4, 3, 2, 1.

Chime In

1. Take children outside to demonstrate flying a kite.
2. Teach the song.
3. Introduce the wall chart.
4. Match words as you sing.
5. Emphasize the quotation marks.
6. Sing the song while the children act as kites.
7. Distribute copies of the song.

Read

When the Wind Stops, Charlotte Zolotov (Harper and Row).

Write

1. Have the children make a title page for their individualized *Chime In* Weather theme books.
2. Some children may make word cards from the song. Others may look in songs to find rhyming words to print on kites. (One word may be printed on the kite body, and rhyming words may be printed on or fastened to the kite tail.)

Physical Education

1. Have the children listen and move to "March Winds" from *Twelve Virtuoso Studies, Opus 46*, Edward MacDowell.
2. Make shapes in the air with crepe paper streamers.
3. Keep a balloon in the air with different parts of the hand.
4. Go for a walk and observe all the things the wind blows. Use a compass to locate North.

Wonder Table

1. Display a compass, mobiles, and wind chimes.
2. Prepare a large chart to show how the wind is helpful and harmful. The children may complete the chart by printing or pasting pictures from newspapers or magazines.

Creative Arts

1. The children will enjoy making boats or kites. For boats, supply scraps of wood, styrofoam, or sheets of aluminum foil (to be folded) and paper and sticks for sails and masts. For kites, provide construction paper, string, and strips of crepe paper (for the tails). Kites may be decorated with scraps of construction paper or gummed shapes.
2. Allow the children to test their boats in the sink or at the water table. Allow them to go outside to fly their kites.

Mathematics

1. Introduce the concept of sequencing. Mark cards with red, blue, and yellow circles in varying orders. Have the children choose cards and decorate their kites with coloured circles in the same sequence.

Chime In

1. Explain that *Sunshine* was the name of a ship blown "right down in town" during a hurricane in the Bahamas. Accompany the song with lively clapping.
2. What else could the wind blow?
3. Introduce the wall chart.
4. Emphasize "-own" sounds.
5. Distribute copies of the song.
6. Have the children add more verses.

Read

The Sun is a Star, Sune Engelbrektson (Holt, Rinehart & Winston).

Write

1. Laminate pictures of wind, and write a sentence for each picture. Have the children match the sentences to the pictures.
2. Make individual Wind books.

Physical Education

1. Parachute activities.
2. Use musical instruments to make a weather story which the children may mime (thunder, rain, lightning, rainbow, sunshine, clouds).

Discuss

1. Discuss safety. Talk about the dangers of thin ice, rushing streams, chasing something that the wind is blowing.

Wonder Table

1. Place a jar of water on the table. Mark the level each day. Where does the water go?
2. Boil a little water. Watch the steam, and note the empty pan.
3. Place one plant in sunlight and one in darkness.
4. Put a piece of blue paper in the sun and another away from the sun.

Creative Arts

1. Have the children paint a rainbow background, make cutouts of other things that make them happy, and paste them on the rainbow.

Mathematics

1. Make a weather graph for March.

WEATHER											
🪁	o	o									
☀	o	o	o	o							
☂	o	o	o	o	o	o					
☁	o	o	o	o	o	o	o	o			
❄	o	o	o								

Visit

1. If possible, take the class to a tall building. Look down at the cars, buildings, and people. Note that things look smaller when they are far away.

Rain

Rain on the green grass,
Rain on the tree,
Rain on the house top,
But not on me.

14

15

Chime In

1. Have the children tap their fingers on the floor to imitate the sound of raindrops as you recite the poem.
2. Introduce the wall chart.
3. Substitute other words for grass, tree, and house.
4. Sing the *Ay Ay* song with "gr-" and "tr-" prefixes (see p. 92).
5. Choose eight children to form pairs and hold up hands to make bridges. The other children march under the bridge while chanting the poem. The bridges try to catch someone on the word *me*.

Read

Rain Drop Splash, Alvin Tresselt (Lothrop, Lee & Shepard).

Write

1. Make raindrop families by cutting out umbrella and raindrop shapes. Pin the shapes on the bulletin board. For example, one umbrella could have the word *green* printed on it. All the raindrops under that umbrella could have words beginning with the same "gr-" blend printed on them.

Mathematics

1. Provide containers of different sizes at the water table. Children may experiment with filling them and comparing the amounts needed to fill them.
2. Put containers of different shapes outside on a rainy day. Have children estimate which container holds the most. Compare them using a standard measure.

Theme Unit 11
Spring

Spring Resource Record

Resources Available	*Comments*
Books and Other Print Materials	
Films, Filmstrips, and Other Non-print Materials	

Resources Available	Comments
Records and Tapes	
People in the Community	
Other (Including Equipment)	

In a Cabin by a Wood

In a cabin by a wood
A little boy by the window stood.
Saw a rabbit hopping by
With some coloured eggs.
"Come on in," the little boy said.
"May I have some green and red?"
"No, oh, no," the rabbit replied.
"It must be a surprise."

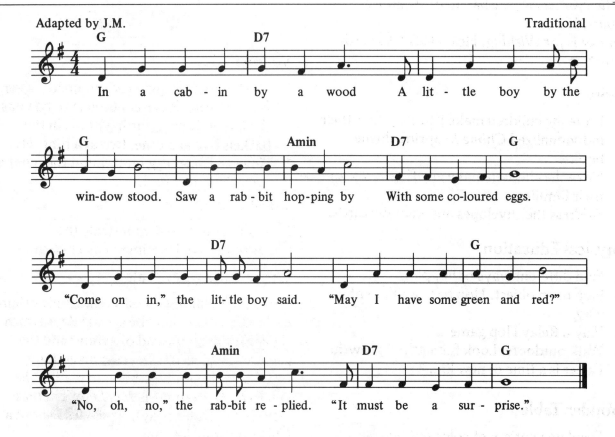

Adapted by J.M.   Traditional

In a cab - in by a wood   A lit - tle boy by the

win-dow stood. Saw a rab - bit hop-ping by   With some co-loured eggs.

"Come on in," the lit- tle boy said.   "May I have some green and red?"

"No, oh, no," the rab-bit re - plied. "It must be a sur - prise."

Chime In

1. Teach the song with an action for each line. For example, shape the cabin with finger tips, shade the eyes, make rabbit ears with the hands.
2. Repeat the song:
   (A) Omit the first line and replace with actions. Sing to the end.
   (B) Omit first and second lines and replace with actions. Sing to the end.
   (C) Omit the first three lines, and so on.
   (D) Continue until you do the entire song with actions only.
   This activity is good preparation for silent reading because the children are thinking about the words in order to do the actions correctly.
3. Introduce the wall chart and sing.
4. Sing often. Add variety by having the children take the parts of the boy, the rabbit, and the narrator.

Read

A Tale for Easter, Tasha Tudor (Henry Z. Wolck, Inc.)
An Egg is for Wishing, Helen Kay (Abelard-Schuman).

Write

1. Have the children make title pages for their individualized *Chime In* Spring theme books.
2. Have the children make greeting cards for their families.
3. Address the envelopes and mail the cards.

Physical Education

1. Find different ways of hopping.
2. Hop to an object. Hop back a different way.
3. Play a Relay Hop game.
4. Walk outdoors. Look for signs of growth. Easter is a time of new life.

Wonder Table

1. Display a variety of coloured eggs.

Creative Arts

1. Make placemats by decorating large construction paper egg shapes with different kinds of lines (thick, thin, straight, curved, jagged).
2. Colour eggs:
   (A) Blow the eggs or hardboil them.
   (B) Wrap in tissue. Close with tape.
   (C) Use an eyedropper or straw to drop two or three colours of dye on each egg.
   (D) Let stand over night.
   (E) Unwrap.
   The colours will have run together, and the children will be curious about the colours on the eggs.
3. Make Easter baskets with this pattern. Fold along the solid lines. Cut along the dotted lines. Paste together the sections marked with solid circles. Add paper handles.

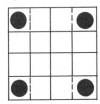

Mathematics

1. Use the baskets and beads to make Easter Bunny treats. Have children take turns as the Easter Bunny, putting beads in the baskets five at a time, two at a time, etc.
2. Have an Easter egg hunt. Limit the number each child may find.

Guest Visit

1. Invite a guest to demonstrate the decoration of Ukrainian Easter eggs.

Other Spring Festivals

If you have children of different ethnic origins in the class, there may be special days which signify for them the end of Winter and the beginning of Spring. Develop an activity, invite a guest, or find a book to read to the children. An example is *Mei Li* by Thomas Handforth (Doubleday), which tells about a Chinese Spring festival.

6

I Know a Little Pussy

I know a little pussy,
Her coat is silver grey,
She lives down in the meadow,
Not very far away.
Although she is a pussy,
She'll never be a cat,
For she's a pussy willow,
Now what do you think of that?
Meow, meow, meow, meow.
Meow, meow, meow, meow, Scat!

7

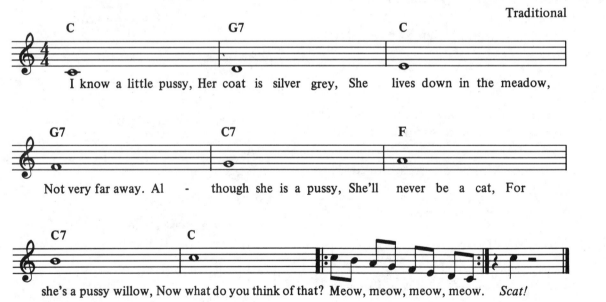

Traditional

C | G7 | C
I know a little pussy, Her coat is silver grey, She lives down in the meadow,

G7 | C7 | F
Not very far away. Al - though she is a pussy, She'll never be a cat, For

C7 | C
she's a pussy willow, Now what do you think of that? Meow, meow, meow, meow. *Scat!*

Chime In

1. Be sure to have some pussy willows in the classroom or take the class outside to examine some.
2. Teach the song with actions (squat, grow gradually). Allow the children to use the xylophone.
3. Start the song softly and gradually sing more loudly. Start the meow's loudly and gradually sing more softly. Then shout *scat*.
4. Emphasize the word *know* (see p.8).
5. Distribute copies of the song.

Weather Calendar

1. Make individual calendars or one for the group. Use symbols or words.

Wonder Table

1. Put some pussy willows in water and some in an empty jar.
2. Put other branches in water, for example, forsythia.

Creative Arts

1. Make pictures of pussy willows using pieces of cotton.

Apple Seed

I'm a little apple seed
Peeking through.
Please help me.
I'll help you.
Dig me a hole
And hide me away,
And I'll be an apple tree
Some fine day.

Chime In

1. Cut an apple. Look at the seeds.
2. Teach the song.
3. Have the children sing with actions.
4. Introduce the wall chart.
5. Emphasize *I'll*, and explain contractions.
6. Distribute copies of the song.

Read

Partouche Plants a Seed, Ben Shecter (Harper and Row).

Write

1. Match sentences:

   I will dig a hole.

   I'll dig a hole.

   He is planting seeds.

   He's planting seeds.

2. Make a story. Copy and illustrate.

Wonder Table

1. Open a bean to see the formation inside.
2. Partially fill a glass with water. Place a lima bean on the inside of the glass above the water line. Hold it in place with a piece of paper that covers the bean and touches the water. (The paper will absorb water and act as an adhesive tape.)

Bluebird, Bluebird

Bluebird, bluebird
Through my window
Bluebird, bluebird
Through my window
Bluebird, bluebird
Through my window
Oh, Johnny, I'm tired.

10

11

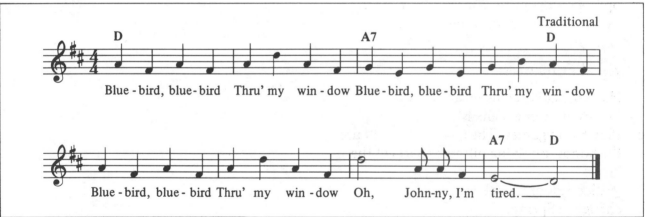

Traditional

Blue-bird, blue-bird Thru' my win-dow Blue-bird, blue-bird Thru' my win-dow

Blue-bird, blue-bird Thru' my win-dow Oh, John-ny, I'm tired.____

Chime In

1. Teach the song as a singing game:
   - (A) The children join hands in a circle.
   - (B) Choose one child to be the bluebird who weaves in and out under their arms.
   - (C) At the words "Oh, Johnny, I'm tired", the bluebird taps another child on the shoulder. This child then becomes the bluebird.
2. Introduce the wall chart and sing.
3. Substitute names of other birds.
4. Sing the *Ay Ay* song using the "thr-" prefix (see p. 92).

Read

Hi! Mister Robin, Alvin Tresselt (Lothrop, Lee & Shepard).

Write

1. Give each child a large petal cutout. Have the child write a sentence or two about Spring on the petal. Mount the petals in flower shapes on the bulletin board.

Physical Education

1. Have the children listen and move to *Voices of Spring*, Felix Mendelssohn.
2. Play Hoop games. The children should use the hoops involving different parts of the body.
3. Walk outdoors. Look for things that change in Spring.

Wonder Table

1. Display a bird's nest and broken shells from hatched eggs.

Creative Arts

1. Make paper bag birds. Stuff bags with paper or fabric scraps. Tie the ends to show a head and tail. Paint, add wings, etc.

Mathematics

1. Play the Hopscotch game.
   - (A) Use carpet tape to outline a hopscotch court and to make the numerals.
   - (B) The children choose number cards to indicate how much they should add to or subtract from each number as they move on the hopscotch court.

I Love the Flowers

I love the flowers.
I love the budding trees.
I love the chirping birds.
I love the buzzing bees.
I love the Springtime,
When the sun is warm and bright.
Boom de-a-da, Boom de-a-da,
Boom de-a-da, Boom,
Boom.

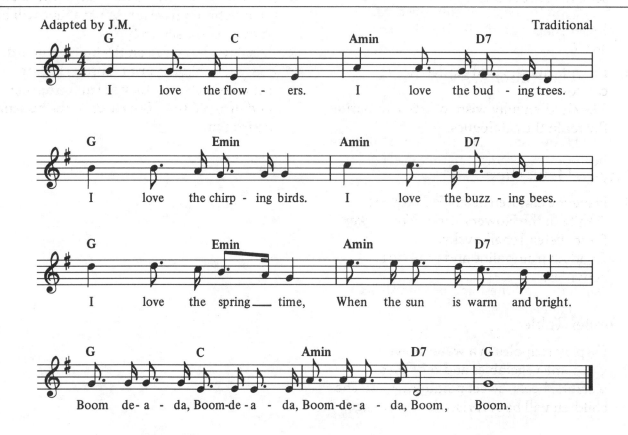

Chime In

1. Collect pictures to represent each line.
2. Teach the song using the pictures to illustrate.
3. Introduce the wall chart and sing.
4. Substitute other objects of love.
5. Play a xylophone accompaniment (GG, EE, AA, DD).

Read

Frogs in a Pond, Little Nature Books, Bill Martin, Jr. (Encyclopedia Britannica).
June Bugs, Little Nature Books, Bill Martin, Jr. (Encyclopedia Britannica).

Write

1. Make a book to illustrate the song by printing one sentence on each page. Note that I love the Springtime/When the sun is warm and bright should be on one page because it is one sentence. The other sentences are shorter.

Display

1. Provide nursery and garden centre catalogues.
2. The children may wish to find a favourite flower in the catalogues.

Physical Education

1. Have the children listen and move to "Waltz of the Flowers" from *Nutcracker Suite*, Peter Tchaikovsky.
2. Conduct trampoline and tumbling activities.

Wonder Table

1. Display tadpoles in a water bowl.
2. Cut some vegetables and root them (carrots, beets, sweet potatoes, etc.). The children will be surprised by the foliage.

Visit

1. If possible, arrange a class visit to a farm where baby animals may be seen.

Gardening

1. Find a place on the school grounds where the children may prepare a garden.

Creative Arts

1. Make a Spring wall hanging.
   (A) Give each child a square of bright cotton on which to pencil a design.
   (B) Stitch the designs with dark wool
   (C) Sew the squares together and back with quilting. (Ask a parent volunteer for help with the sewing.)

Mathematics

1. Have the children trace the bases of various sizes of cylindrical shapes. Then have them put the objects which they have traced on an overhead projector. What shape will be shown on the screen?
2. Display a large sun on the bulletin board. Have the children print word cards for round objects that they see in the Spring and then pin the word cards to the bulletin board sun.

The Little Robin

There was a little robin
Whose head was always bobbin'
Who said, as he gobbled up a worm,
"I have swallowed all your brothers
And thirty-seven others
And goodness how they tickle
When they squirm."

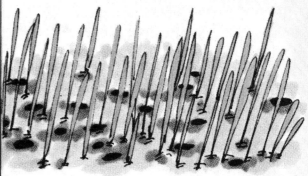

14

15

Chime In

1. Go for a walk. Observe a robin.
2. Teach the poem.
3. Divide class into two groups, narrators and robins.
4. Introduce the wall chart.
5. Emphasize the quotation marks and "th" sound (tongue-cooler).
6. Make substitutes in the *Lappy Lappy* song (see p. 60).

Write

1. Some children will be ready to begin a research project on birds or worms (see p. 9).
2. Others may make word cards from the poem.
3. Some children could write other things that the robin said as it gobbled up a worm.

Wonder Table

1. Place some worms in a jar of sand. Wrap the jar with black paper.
2. Remove the paper and observe the castings.

Creative Arts

1. Stuff an old nylon with paper or fabric scraps to make a giant worm. Add features and give it a name.

Mathematics

1. Use shoelaces or lengths of string to make groups of ten worms. Count by 10's.

Examine

1. Look at worms under hand lenses.
2. Predict what worms will do under certain conditions. (What will it do if I put a block in its path?)

Theme Unit 12
My Family

My Family Resource Record

Resources Available	Comments
Books and Other Print Materials	
Films, Filmstrips, and Other Non-print Materials	

Resources Available	Comments
Records and Tapes	
People in the Community	
Other (Including Equipment)	

Ten in the Bed

Ten in the bed and the little one said,
   "Roll over, roll over."
  They all rolled over and one fell out.
Nine in the bed and the little one said,
   "Roll over, roll over."
  They all rolled over and one fell out.

Eight....
Seven....
Six....
Five....
Four....
Three....
Two....
One in the bed and the little one said,
   "Alone at last!"

4

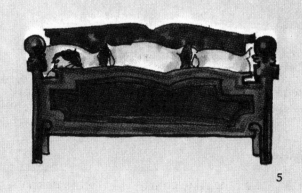

5

Traditional

F

Ten   in   the bed   and   the   lit - tle one   said, "Roll   o   -   ver,   roll

o   -   ver."   They all   rolled   o - ver and   one   fell   out.

Chime In

1. Sing the song.
2. Have children play the autoharp accompaniment (only one chord is needed).
3. Divide the class into groups of ten and sing with actions.
4. Add verses, such as Ten in the pool.
5. Introduce the wall chart, and read the song.
6. Emphasize the "-ed" suffix (roll, rolled).
7. Distribute copies of the song.

Read

Bedtime for Francis, Russell Hoban (Harper and Row).
Great-Grandfather, the Baby and Me, Howard Knotts (McClelland & Stewart).

Write

1. Make a language chart of words to describe mothers.
2. Have the children make Mother's Day cards.

Physical Education

1. Have the children listen and relax to "Children's Prayer" from *Hansel and Gretel*, Engelbert Humperdinck.

Picture Study

1. Ask parents to lend some of their family pictures. The children may tell the class about their families as the pictures are viewed.

Make Gifts

1. Make felt wall hangings.
   (A) Give each child a rectangular piece of felt to decorate with felt scraps, ribbon, or other materials.
   (B) Add coloured wool or ribbon for hanging. Centre the wool or ribbon across the back 1 cm from the top edge. Spread white glue over the top of the felt for 1 cm and fold the felt over to cover the wool or ribbon string.
   (C) The children may take their wall hangings home as Mother's Day gifts or for some other occasion.

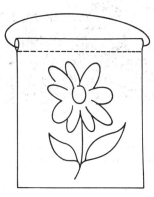

Creative Arts

1. Make a finger puppet family.
   (A) Draw figures (body and head) on heavy paper and cut them out.
   (B) Add features.
   (C) Cut two holes for legs.
   (D) Put fingers through the holes to do the walking.

Mathematics

1. Tell addition and subtraction stories.
   (A) Make number cards with a drawing of a bed on each one.
   (B) The children will make pillows with number stories to match the card number. For example, the number card 6 could have pillows with 3 + 3, 4 + 2, 8 − 2, etc.

My Father Is a Butcher

My Father is a butcher.
My Mother cuts the meat.
And I'm a little hot dog
That runs around the street.

6

Chime In

1. Present a variety of pictures showing men and women in different occupations.
2. Teach the poem.
3. Have one group add sound effects (such as chanting "chop, chop") while others repeat the poem.
4. Introduce the wall chart and read the poem.
5. What else could father be? What else could mother be?

Read

If It Weren't for You, Charlotte Zolotov (Harper and Row).

Write

1. Have the children make a title page for their individualized *Chime In* My Family theme books.
2. Write stories about different occupations.
   (A) Tape sounds of different occupations (carpenter, dentist, musician, farmer, welder, and so on).
   (B) Collect pictures to illustrate different occupations.
   (C) Have the children listen to the tape and arrange the pictures in sequence.
   (D) Have the children write a sentence for each picture.
3. Have each child write and illustrate a page entitled When I Grow Up. Make a class book with these pages.

Story Telling

1. Make flannel board family figures.
   (A) The children may cut out pictures of other articles they need for their stories, paste them on flannel, and cut them out. Examples are trucks, typewriters, buildings.
   (B) Have the children make up stories about the flannel board families to tell to their friends.

Physical Education

1. Play the Did You Ever game.
   (A) Sing to the tune of *Did You Ever See a Lassie?* Use different lyrics. (Did you ever see a father? a mother? a sister? a brother?)
   (B) The children form a circle. One child stands in the centre and mimes the action of the father, mother, and so on.
   (C) On the words Go this way. . . , the other children imitate the action being mimed.

Discuss

1. Talk about how members of a family help each other.
2. Demonstrate helping with puppets and with drama (provide dress-up clothes).
3. Make a chart of tasks children can do at home. Put the names of the children on word cards to clip by the tasks. The names may then be easily changed as the children report on how they have helped.

Creative Arts

1. Have the children colour pictures of the members of their families at work. Mount them on the bulletin board in a circular collage display. Around the outside of the circle, print the words of the poem.
2. Have the children paint pictures of their family.

Mathematics

1. Make Family bar graphs.
   (A) Have the children bring in strips of paper indicating the length of each family member's foot. (Wallpaper is ideal.)
   (B) The children will then arrange and glue the strips on large sheets of paper and decorate with shoe pictures cut from magazines.

Mabel, Mabel

Mabel, Mabel
Set the table.
Don't forget the
Salt, mustard, vinegar, pepper,
Salt, mustard, vinegar, pepper.

7

Chime In

1. This poem is a skipping rhyme. Repeat the last line more and more quickly.
2. Use the poem with skipping ropes in the playground or the gym.
3. Introduce the wall chart. Read it with the class.
4. Change the last line.
5. Have the children take turns covering the last line with the ones they have printed.

Read

Sand Cake, Frank Asch (Parents' Magazine Press).

Write

1. Use newspaper ads, menus, or articles from the store to make up new verses.

Creative Arts

1. Make paper placemats.
   (A) Cut a green pepper in half. Dip it in paint and stamp it on paper. Or paint a cabbage leaf and press it on paper. These and other vegetables make interesting designs for the placemats.
   (B) Fringe the edges.

Mathematics

1. Have the children set the table for a given number.
2. Make plasticene fruit, and cut in halves and quarters.

My Puppy

I think it's very funny
The way a puppy grows
A little on his wiggly tail
A little on his nose
A little on his tummy
A little on his ears
I guess he'll be a dog all right
In half a dozen years.

8

Chime In

1. Discuss different kinds of pets and the care of pets.
2. Teach the poem, using actions.
3. Introduce the wall chart and read the poem together.
4. Emphasize the "-le" suffix by changing the *Lappy Lappy* song to *Lapple Lapple* (see p. 60).
5. Distribute copies of the poem.

Read

Old Arthur, Liesel Skorpen (Harper and Row). *Angus and the Ducks*, Marjorie Flack (Doubleday).

Write

1. The children may add a page to their theme books with a story or picture about their pets.
2. Cut out pictures telling a "pet story". Have children arrange them in sequence and write or tell the story.

Physical Education

1. Have the children move like puppies.
   (A) Have them listen for and respond to commands, such as sit, stay, beg, down, there, roll over.
   (B) Substitute word cards for verbal commands.

Drama

1. Place a leash and a dog's dish in the play area.

Mathematics

1. Develop the concept of half a dozen. Have the children model half a dozen objects, such as eggs or oranges. Use half of an egg carton for storage and display.

Visit

1. If possible visit a pet shop or a pet show. If possible, buy a pet for the class.

Fire! Fire!

Fire! Fire! Fire! Fire!
Hear the siren blowing.
Fire! Fire! Fire! Fire!
Firefighters are going
To climb the ladder
And squirt the hose.
With a sh, sh, sh, sh,
Out the fire goes.

9

Chime In

1. Discuss safety at home.
2. Teach the song with actions.
3. Add sound effects, such as cymbals for Fire! Fire! and sand blocks for sh, sh.
4. Introduce the wall chart and sing the song together.
5. Distribute copies of the song.

Read

Fire! Fire! said Mrs. McGuire, Instant Reader, Bill Martin, Jr. (Holt, Rinehart & Winston).

Visit

1. Take the class on a tour of a fire station.
2. While there, take photographs for presentation later.
3. Have the children make a tape to accompany the photographs.
4. Give the children stickers showing the phone number of the fire department.

Drama

1. In the play area, put a firefighter's hat, a short hose, large blocks, and a telephone.

Physical Education

1. Use the climbing apparatus so that the children may pretend to be firefighters climbing ladders and sliding down poles.
2. For rope activities:
   (A) Scatter equipment around the gym.
   (B) Have a child hook his or her rope on to one piece of equipment and move around the other pieces.
   (C) Blindfold the child and have him or her use the rope to find the way back to the piece of equipment attached to the rope.

Theme Unit 13
Summer Fun

Summer Fun Resource Record

Resources Available	*Comments*
Books and Other Print Materials	
Films, Filmstrips, and Other Non-print Materials	

Resources Available	*Comments*
Records and Tapes	
People in the Community	
Other (Including Equipment)	

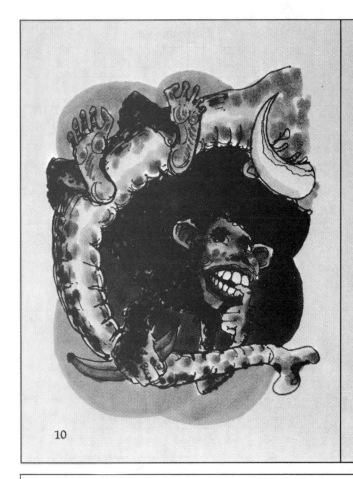

The Animal Fair

I went to the animal fair.
The birds and the beasts were there.
The big baboon by the light of the moon
Was combing his auburn hair.
You ought to have seen the monk.
He jumped on the elephant's trunk.
The elephant sneezed,
Fell down on his knees,
And that was the end of the monk,
        the monk.

10

11

American Song

I went to the an - i - mal fair. _____ The birds and the beasts were

there. _____ The big ba - boon by the light of the moon Was

comb - ing his au - burn hair. _____ You ought to have seen the

monk. _____ He jumped on the el - e - phant's trunk. _____ The

el-e-phant sneezed, Fell down on his knees, And that was the end of the monk, the monk.

Chime In

1. Teach the song, using pictures of animals.
2. Divide the class into two groups. Have one group continue chanting "the monk, the monk" as the other sings the song. Accompany with instruments.
3. Introduce the wall chart and sing together.
4. Match words as they sing.
5. Distribute copies of the song.

Read

You Look Ridiculous Said the Rhinoceros to the Hippopotamus, Bernard Wabe (Houghton-Mifflin).

Write

1. Give each child an invitation to a birthday party at the zoo.
2. Have them write a reply.
3. Have them make a shopping list for presents.

The Zoo

We are going to the zoo,
To the zoo, to the zoo.
We are going to the zoo.
Won't you come along?

We will see the elephants,
Elephants, elephants.
We will see the elephants.
Won't you come along?

12

J.M.   Traditional

We are go - ing to the zoo, To the zoo, to the zoo.

We are go - ing to the zoo. Won't you come a - long?

Chime In

1. Dramatize the song in the gym.
2. Discuss means of transportation to the zoo (bus, car, train).
3. Have the children suggest what animals they might see at the zoo.
4. Dramatize their suggestions.
5. Introduce the wall chart.
6. Make word cards for other animals to make substitute verses.
7. Distribute copies of the song.

Read

May I Bring a Friend,
Beatrice de Regniers (Atheneum).
I Was Kissed by a Seal at the Zoo,
Helen Palmer (Beginner Books).

Write

1. Have the children make a title page for their individualized *Chime In* Summer Fun theme books.
2. Have the children write more verses for the song and illustrate them.
3. Allow those who are ready to do research on one of the animals.
4. Have the children write a letter to a friend telling of the trip to the zoo. (Provide pictures as a guide.)

Physical Education

1. Have the children listen and move to *Le Carnaval des Animaux*, Camille Saint-Saëns.
2. Play the Rope Cage game. Have a group of children hold on to a rope. Form the rope into a round cage, a square cage, a triangular cage, and so on. Have a child in the centre mime an animal. The children forming the rope cage must guess what animal is being mimed.

3. Use various instruments to improvise sounds to represent different animals. Have the children respond by miming the animals' actions.

Visit

1. If possible, take the class on a visit to a zoo. While there, take photographs of the animals and tape the sounds they make.
2. Play the tape later, and have the children guess which animal is making the sound. Use the photographs.

Creative Arts

1. Cut tissue paper shapes. Interesting designs may be made by overlapping and pasting the shapes.
2. Build three-dimensional "cages" with straws. Join the straws by putting a small piece of pipe cleaner in the ends of two straws to be joined.
3. Make a frieze of animal models. Make trees, etc., and set up the frieze in the sand table.

Mathematics

1. Provide picture cards or plastic animals for sorting into sets. Explain the sorting rule (water or land animals, animals from hot or cold climates, by colour, by size, and so on). At evaluation time, the children should take turns explaining their sorting rule. As they mention each animal, they should place it on the overhead projector. Keep the projector far enough from the screen so that the image will be life size.

My Nice New Bike

Come and see my nice new bike,
Nice new bike, nice new bike.
Come and see my nice new bike.
Would you like a ride?

Hear the bell go ding, ding, ding,
Ding, ding, ding, ding, ding, ding.
Hear the bell go ding, ding, ding,
Would you like a ride?

13

Traditional
Tune: Mulberry Bush

J.M.

G   D7

Come and see   my nice   new bike,   Nice   new bike,   Nice   new bike.

G   D7   G

Come   and see   my nice   new bike.   Would   you like   a   ride?

Chime In

1. Show a bicycle bell.
2. Sing the song. Have a child ring the bell at the appropriate times.
3. Introduce the wall chart.
4. Add more verses, such as See the wheels go round and round.
5. Distribute copies of the song.

Read

Curious George Rides a Bike, Margaret Rey (Houghton-Mifflin).

Discuss

1. Talk about sharing and caring for toys.

Mathematics

Give each child a variety of attribute blocks.
1. Have each child select one block. Then have the children exchange the one they have chosen by changing its
   (A) shape,
   (B) colour,
   (C) size.
2. Pair the children. One child should make a design with the blocks. The partner then copies the design.

Guest Visit

1. Invite a librarian to speak to the parents and the children about summer activities at the public library.

Watch

Show *Danced Squared*.

Physical Education

Discuss body shapes.
1. Have the children travel about the floor, making different shapes as they move.
2. Have the children jump from a standing position, showing:
   (A) a wide shape,
   (B) a long, thin shape,
   (C) a rounded shape,
   (D) a twisted shape.
3. Using apparatus, have the children:
   (A) travel on the equipment, keeping their body in one shape,
   (B) make a shape in the air as they get off.

Going on a Picnic

Going on a picnic,
Leaving right away.
If it doesn't rain,
We'll stay all day.

Did you bring the hot dogs?
Yes, I brought the hot dogs.
Did you bring the salad?
Yes, I brought the salad.
Ready for a picnic
Here we go.

14

Lynn Freeman Olson

Go - ing on   a pic - nic,   Leav - ing right   a - way.

If   it does - n't rain,   We'll   stay   all   day.

Did   you bring the hot dogs?   Yes,   I brought the hot dogs.
sal - ad?   sal - ad.

Read - y for   a pic - nic   Here   we   go.

Chime In

1. Use a picnic hamper and contents to illustrate the song.
2. Have the children develop other questions and answers.
3. Introduce and sing with the wall chart.
4. Emphasize the question marks.
5. Have the children print their questions on a long strip of paper to replace the questions on the wall chart.
6. Distribute copies of the song.

Read

A Salmon for Simon, Betty Waterton (Douglas & McIntyre).
Euphonia and the Flood, Mary Calhoun (Parents' Magazine Press).

Write

1. Have the children add more verses to their theme books.
2. Pack a picnic hamper and leave it in the writing centre. The children write lists of things that might be in it. At the end of the activity period, have one child open the hamper. The children then check their lists to see who made the greatest number of correct guesses.

Physical Education

1. Discuss water safety when swimming.
2. Have the children listen and relax to *Ebb Tide*, Maxwell and Sigman.
3. Play the Going on a Picnic game using the Bear Hunt game format (see p. 75).

Wonder Table

1. Provide a variety of shells and pebbles. Display books about shell and rock collections.

2. As an alternate or as an additional activity, provide a magnet and a number of objects that the magnet will and will not pick up. The children may record their observations on individual charts.

Drama

1. Place a picnic hamper in the play area. It should have plastic containers, a tablecloth, thermos, utensils, and so on.

Plan a Picnic

1. Have the children make invitations for their parents. (The picnic may be held on the school grounds. Going a distance is not important for children.)
2. Have the children mix lemonade and make and wrap sandwiches for the picnic.

Creative Arts

1. Make animals with stones and pieces of felt, wood, etc., or add features by painting.
2. Finger paint while listening to *Ebb Tide*. Have the children move their fingers and hands to the music.

Mathematics

1. Play the Fishing game.
   (A) Make construction paper fish.
   (B) Print an addition or subtraction question on each fish.
   (C) Print the answer on another piece of paper and paper clip it to the appropriate fish. Turn the answer to the inside so that the children can't see it.
   (D) Make a fishing rod with a magnet as a hook.
   (E) The children take turns fishing. They answer the questions they "catch" and then check the answers.

Swinging

Swinging in the swing,
Swinging up so high,
We can almost bump our heads.
Up against the sky.

15

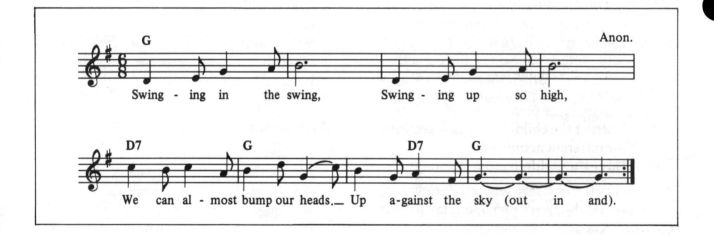

Swing - ing in   the swing,   Swing - ing up   so high,

We can al - most bump our heads.__ Up a-gainst the sky (out   in   and).

Anon.

Chime In

1. Teach the song as a game:
   - (A) Divide the class into groups of three.
   - (B) Two of each group join hands to form a swing. The third child stands within the swing formed.
   - (C) The groups themselves form one large circle.
   - (D) The pairs joining hands swing their arms forward and back while singing the song.
   - (E) On the word *sky*, the child in the swing moves out of that swing and into the next one. Be sure to have all the children in the swings facing in the same direction.
2. Distribute copies of the song.

Read

Never Say Ugh! to a Bug, Norma Farber (Greenwillow Publishers).
What I Like About Toads, Judy Howes (Thomas Y. Crowell).

Write

1. Have each child make a plan for a playground.
   - (A) Supply large pieces of paper.
   - (B) Instruct the children to mark sections for different activities.
   - (C) Have the children put a sign on each activity section.

Wonder Table

1. Provide balance scales and a variety of objects to weigh.

Physical Education

1. Develop body awareness by distributing weight on different body parts. Have the children place all their weight on one foot, on their shoulders, on one hand and foot, etc.

Mathematics

1. Play the Weighing game. Record the mass of a variety of objects.
2. Use balance scales to compare masses. Prepare two charts, one headed Greater Than and one headed Less Than. The children should record their findings on the appropriate chart. For example, the book has a mass greater than the puzzle. The puzzle has a mass less than the book, toy truck, and so on.

Index